The Cheerful Giver

The Cheerful Giver

Essays

BY

SAMUEL McCHORD CROTHERS

Essay Index Reprint Series

BOOKS FOR LIBRARIES PRESS
FREEPORT, NEW YORK

PS3505
R9C5

INTERNATIONAL STANDARD BOOK NUMBER:
0-8369-2389-8

LIBRARY OF CONGRESS CATALOG CARD NUMBER:
73-156634

PRINTED IN THE UNITED STATES OF AMERICA
BY
NEW WORLD BOOK MANUFACTURING CO., INC.
HALLANDALE, FLORIDA 33009

CONTENTS

THE CHEERFUL GIVER

"The Lord loveth a cheerful giver"; and so do we all. Especially is this true of those who give us their opinions. Perhaps one might say that it is only when these unsolicited donations are made in a cheerful manner that they are tolerated. When a person offers us a piece of his mind, we suspect him of hostile intent. The history of the word "gratuitous" is enlightening. Its primary definition is, "freely bestowed or obtained; costing nothing." Its secondary meaning is, "unnecessary, uncalled for; as, a gratuitous insult."

In a certain sense all expression of opinion is gratuitous. It is uncalled for. Especially is this true if the opinion offered conflicts with one which is already held. People usually prefer their own opinions to those that are recommended by outsiders. They may not be of the most advanced kind, but they are more comfortable to live with.

The insistence on cheerfulness does not apply to professional advisers like lawyers, doctors, architects, engineers, and the like. These experts do not give us their advice: they allow us to buy it from them. We do not expect them to be in high spirits when we go to them in office hours. Even though they be "sad-hearted men much overgone with care," we accept their opinions meekly. We will allow a psychoanalyst with austere countenance to tell us the most devastating truths about ourselves. But let no candid friend offer us the same information gratuitously.

Let all idealists, reformers, philanthropists, friendly visitors, people with causes they wish to promote, and all who would give good advice without charging a fee, remember this. There is a temperamental quality needed to make their gifts acceptable. Chaucer's Clerke of Oxenforde in spite of his solemn ways, had learned the secret: "gladly wolde he lerne and gladly teche." Even the Wife of Bath would tolerate his didacticism when she saw how much pleasure he got out of it.

This is not to say that we should give a hearing only to those who insist on looking always on the bright side of things. The dark side must be faced also, but we do not care for the mind that sheds new darkness upon it. A defeatist is never so unwelcome as when the tide of battle is going against us. The facts are threatening enough, but why surrender to them so abjectly?

The leaders of forlorn hopes are never found among men with dismal minds. There must be a natural resiliency of temper which makes them enjoy desperate ventures. Ignatius Loyola, who had an uncanny skill in picking winners in the race for martyrdom, was always on the lookout for high-spirited young men with a keen zest for life. When he heard that a young Spaniard, Francis Xavier, was astonishing Paris by his gayety, he spared no pains to convert him. He was just the man he was looking for. He wanted some one to go through shipwrecks and famines and persecutions as one who rejoiced in tribulation.

The biographers of Xavier, while narrating his unparalleled sufferings, find the miraculous element in his constant good cheer. He set forth on the missionary enterprise from which he was never to return "light of heart and joyful in discourse." When others wept, we are told, "the countenance of Xavier alone beamed with delight." On the overcrowded and fever-stricken ship from Lisbon to Goa, Xavier, clothed in rags, was the life of the company. When the soldiers gambled on the deck, he held the stakes for which they played in order that he might win them by his gay discourse from further excesses. He mingled freely with all classes and entered into their interests.

When he reached Goa, he knew nothing of the language of the people whom he had come to convert, but, swinging a hand bell, he went through the streets calling to repentance. Soon all the children of Goa were following this smiling John the Baptist. In a little while, their parents were asking, "What went ye out for to see?" Their curiosity was excited and they were eager to know what this emaciated, barefooted stranger found in Goa to smile about. Then, when he offered them baptism, they took it. How could they help it?

I think that a great deal of history is misconceived because historians, being often of sedentary habits and being dependent on documents, have not taken sufficient account of the part which temperament plays in human affairs. They fix their attention on the policies for which a great man stands rather than upon the characteristics which induce other people to accept from him what they would reject from others. The great man is a leader of men, not a driver. A leader is one who has the power to induce other people to follow him.

What is the nature of that power? I think it may be best defined as the attraction of gravitation. It inheres in sheer bulk. It is the attraction which the greater has for the less. We are not drawn to one who is meagerly endowed with an excellent quality. We follow one who has enough and to spare.

What was it that made men follow Oliver Cromwell and take at his hands that which they would not receive from any of his contemporaries? Most of the historians of the period give little hint of this attractive power. I cannot find it in the reports of the long, rambling speeches that are preserved. But a chance remark of Richard Baxter, who had many opportunities of meeting him, throws light upon the man. "He was a man of excellent natural parts for affection and oratory, but not well seen in the principles of his religion: of a sanguine complexion, naturally of such a vivacity, hilarity, and alacrity as another man hath when he hath drunken a cup too much."

There you have it. Oliver Cromwell had what the other men of his party had, but he had more of it. You might know Puritanism of the ordinary sort and yet not know the charm that was in the personality of this hearty Englishman. In him Puritanism was consistent with an unusual amount of vivacity, hilarity, and alacrity. So long as Stout Oliver lived, the Commonwealth endured. When the right-minded, neutral-tinted Richard Cromwell became Lord Protector, the Cromwellian charm was broken, and the hearts of the people turned toward the Merry Monarch.

We may lament this fickleness of the crowd, which insists on following those who seem to have found something that gives them satisfaction. It is like the instinct which makes little chickens follow that one of their number who indicates by his joyful demeanor that he has found the fattest worm. Though "vivacity, hilarity, and alacrity" may be looked upon as gifts of Nature rather than of grace, they serve to make the higher gifts acceptable.

The metallurgist dealing with refractory ores finds substances which will not fuse in the hottest furnace unless he introduces some substance that acts as a flux. Cheerfulness is in ethics what fluorspar is in metallurgy. It is a flux absolutely necessary in dealing with refractory moral elements.

In the following essays I have not concealed my sympathy with those who, like Shelley, have "a passion for reforming the world." But if they are to succeed even moderately in their undertaking, they must be prepared to deal with many refractory elements. The fact is that the world does not care to be reformed. It prefers to muddle along as it has done for many millenniums. This makes the way of the improver hard.

All the more need, then, that he should have a store of good humor which will carry him through the days when the world is recalcitrant or even oblivious of his labors in its behalf. I do not like to see him waste his time in needless worries and grow querulous before his time.

I address myself, therefore, to the problems of those who do not need to be persuaded to be givers, but who are sometimes in doubt whether in such a world as this they have a right to be cheerful. They are convinced of their social responsibilities, but they would like some suggestions as to the way to distribute the load so that it shall not crush them. For such persons the question of leisure demands attention. They may be sure that in this industrial era their work will find them out; but the secret of enjoying their work is something which they must find out for themselves.

LEISURE WHILE YOU WAIT

Much has been written in praise of leisure. Leisurely writing and leisurely reading have been commended as good for the soul's health. The mind should not always be on the stretch, but there should be intervals in which we should do no manner of work; at least any that imposed upon us. The intellect should have leisure to refresh itself at the fountain head. It should not be made a wheezy pump to lift water from a half-filled cistern. There should be a sense of effortless abundance.

To all this we agree, but there is one consideration that causes pain. The cultivation of leisure seems to take a great deal of time.

"The wisdom of the learned man," says the son of Sirach, "cometh by the opportunity of leisure, and he that hath little business shall be wise." He then turns to those who do not belong to the leisure class, and quenches their aspirations after wisdom. It is a luxury that is beyond their station in life.

"How can he get wisdom that holdeth the

plough and glorieth in the goad, that driveth oxen and is occupied in their labors, and whose talk is bullocks? So is every carpenter and work master that laboreth day and night. The smith also sitting by the anvil and considering the iron work and fighting with the heat of the furnace." In no better plight is "the potter sitting at his work, and turning the wheel with his feet, and his eyes look still upon the pattern of the thing that he maketh."

All these busy people, he says, are necessary. Without them the city cannot be inhabited. "They maintain the state of the world and their desire is in the work of their hands." They are very useful, very indispensable, but they have not leisure to grow wise. Their minds cannot ripen properly. "They cannot declare justice and judgment, and they shall not be found where parables are spoken."

This is so, but it is not the whole story. Skilled artisans are not the only persons who suffer from the lack of the opportunities of leisure. The intellectual classes, as their interests become highly specialized, find it difficult to give their minds free play. One who aims at what is called "productive scholarship" has not the

time to sit at ease "where parables are spoken."
The parable must be cut short. If only he who
has little business shall be wise, then there is
small hope for the University Professor. Wherein
does the potter, turning the wheel with his foot
while his eyes look still upon the pattern of the
thing that he maketh, differ from the harassed
candidate for a Ph.D. degree, as he looks at the
pattern of the thesis that he maketh? Wherein
does a society of scholars whose tasks are set
by an efficiency expert differ from any other
well-organized body of industrialists? It is hard
to evade the consequences of all work and no
play.

It is our habit to think of everything in terms
of big business, and yet there are times when we
rebel against the creed that the whole duty of
man is to keep busy. Surely we were not born to
spend our lives in involuntary servitude. It
must be right now and then to do as we please.
But how can we find time for such laudable tru-
ancies? That is what causes anxious thought.

There is a letter of Cornelius Fronto to his pupil, Marcus Aurelius Antoninus, which takes up
this matter from the standpoint of health. The
young Emperor's conscience was a taskmaster

demanding continual toil. Fronto reminds him that it is possible for one with the best intentions to destroy his own powers for usefulness by over-strain.

"What do circumstances demand of you? Not study, not toil, not duties. What bow is forever strung?"

He suggests to him that the very best service he could render to the Roman Empire would be that he should get into such a state of mind that after each day's work he would be sure of a good night's sleep. He urges him not to look upon his duties with a prolonged stare. "Learn to wink." It was good advice for the serious Stoic. "Remember your father, that godlike man who excelled others in continence and righteousness, yet he knew how to relax. He baited a hook and laughed at buffoons."

Then Fronto put his good advice in the form of an apologue. In the beginning, Father Jove divided man's life into two parts and gave equal value to both. The day he assigned to work, the night to rest. But he did not think of creating sleep, for he took it for granted that every one would be wise enough to rest while awake.

But little by little business began to encroach

on the time allotted to rest, and both gods and men fell into the bad habit of turning night into day. First Neptune complained of fatigue. The waves, he said, were so restless that he was kept busy all the time in the attempt to control them and to keep them from encroaching on the shore.

Pluto reported that Hades was so crowded and disturbed that he had no leisure for his own meditations. "He had a watchdog to terrify any shades that tried to escape. It had three throats for barking, three gaping jaws, and three sets of terrible teeth; still he was so anxious over what might happen that he could get no rest."

"Then Jupiter questioned the other gods and found that they were turning night into day. So Jupiter created Sleep, and set him in charge of the night." There must be a time when men might "forget the whirling of chariots and the thunder of steeds." Fronto advises Marcus to learn to sleep till such time as he can learn to rest during his waking hours.

The reply of Marcus Aurelius to this advice is written in the tone of the tired business man: "*To my master Fronto, greeting.*

"I have just received your letter, which I will enjoy presently. But for the moment I have duties hanging over me that cannot be begged off. Meanwhile, I am very busy."

Then by way of postscript he adds: "After dictating the above, I read the letter while the others were dining. I shall read it often, that I may know how to rest. But you know how exacting duty is."

That notion that leisure is a luxury forbidden to people who work with their hands or brains, is denied by those who hold that it is a state of mind, not dependent on particular circumstances. It is possible to cultivate this state of mind, and it doesn't take so much time as some people suppose. Saint Paul, writing to the Thessalonians, says, "Study to be quiet." This is a mental exercise much to be commended to Americans. But Paul looked upon it as quite compatible with one's ordinary activities. His exhortation to restfulness is followed by a commendation of the industrial virtues. "Study to be quiet, and to do your own business, and to work with your own hands."

People who complain of the high cost of leisure at the present time are apt to look back with futile regret to some golden age which has forever passed. How restful to have lived in the days of

Charles Lamb, when one could browse among old books and enjoy his own thoughts without looking at the clock!

But one has doubts as he reads a letter of Lamb to his friend Wordsworth. It would indicate that leisure was not always had for the asking, even by one so capable of appreciating it:

"*My dear W.*: I have scarce time or quiet to explain my present situation, how unquiet and distracted it is, owing to the absence of some of my compeers, and to the deficient state of payments in the E. I. H. owing to bad peace speculations in the calico market!"

He is compelled to work nights in order to catch up with the accumulation of business. "The nature of my work, too, puzzling and hurrying, has so shaken my spirits that my sleep is nothing but a succession of dreams of business I cannot do, of assistants that give me no assistance, of terrible responsibilities.... I see no prospect of a quiet day, or hour even, till this week and the next are past."

That sounds very familiar. But in parentheses Lamb lets us into a secret that relieves the situation. He says, "(I write this to W. W. Esq., Collector of Stamp Duties for the conjoint

Northern Counties, not W. W. Poet.)" While
the clerk at India House and the collector of
stamps for the "conjoint Northern Counties"
were complaining of being overworked, the author of the "Excursion" and the author of the
"Essays of Elia" were not greatly affected.
They were prepared to enjoy bits of time which
were not devoted to business purposes. Wordsworth, indeed, succeeded in getting a good deal
of time for his own uses, but Lamb had to do his
meditating on London streets. So one may see a
beauty-loving railway section hand cultivating
his little flower garden on "the right of way."
The company doesn't mind, and it gives him a
real pleasure.

Speaking of the "right of way" reminds me
that the word "leisure" is derived from the
Latin, *licere*, to be permitted, and is connected
with our word "license." It implies that we are
permitted to do something for our own pleasure
in time not needed for strictly utilitarian uses.
We are allowed to cultivate the right of way, so
long as these adornments do not interfere with
the passage of the trains. So Sir Thomas Browne
found time in hours not taken up by his medical
practice to jot down some thoughts that had

pleased him. He says of his book that it was something that "I had at leisurable hours composed." These leisurable hours do not always come in large pieces. Leisure is often more highly valued when it must be taken in installments.

The number of these leisurable hours that any one has at his disposal is limited, and their distribution throughout a lifetime is often beyond the control of the individual. William Penn's "Fruits of Solitude" was the result of a season of forced retirement. But Penn was a very wealthy man, and, besides, was a Quaker. He may be looked upon as a plutocrat in the way of leisure. Most of us must get our solitude in broken lots.

Yet it is remarkable how many opportunities for leisure one can find if he is on the lookout for them. We are told that even an atom is more roomy than one would imagine. An electron moves about in its vast spaces like a lonely planet. And one can get a good deal of aloneness in a minute. Our thoughts need not be hurried or crowded if each is allowed to take its moment when it comes. There are fragments of time that come from broken engagements. There are periods of salutary waiting; waiting for street cars, and dentists, and committees whose chairmen have been delayed by other committees. There are moments in the busiest day when through no fault of our own we are left accidentally alone. There may not be time in these chance intervals for the choicer fruits of solitude to ripen, but there is at least time for some mushroom growths. The punctual man has many such moments for solitary musing while he is waiting for the unpunctual man.

The mind is its own place and in itself can create a driven feeling in the Vale of Arcady. And where is there more calm repose than in the mind of the officer at Fifth Avenue and Forty-Second Street, as he deliberately moves his hands, like Moses at the Red Sea, dividing the waves of traffic that the hurried people may pass in safety?

To take advantage of these fleeting opportunities, one must have a quick control over his own mind. He must not only be able to start his mental machinery, but he must be able to stop it when it is moving to no purpose. This is the more difficult matter. Many persons keep their minds revolving ceaselessly on one subject for the same reason that the driver of a temperamental automobile lets his engine run while the car stops. He is afraid that if it gets cool he can't crank it again. A reliable self-starter would save a great deal of wear and tear.

I cannot include under the pleasant name of "leisure" those activities that are carried on systematically after business hours. Very soon they become things that *must* be done. There are misers of time who clutch at each spare moment and put it to usury. They expect some definite return from their investment. All mental activities which are closely articulated and planned in advance should be classed under the head of "overtime work." In our moments of true leisure the unexpected happens, or, if nothing happens, we do not care. We do that which is unprofitable because it pleases us. We read a book because it happens to be near us and it looks inviting. It is a case where propinquity is everything. The latchstring of the mind is out. We entertain random thoughts and are occasionally surprised to find that we have entertained wisdom unawares. Our attitude is like that of Elizabeth's great minister, Lord Burleigh, who at the end of a day's work would fling his robe of office on the floor and say, "Lie there, my Lord Treasurer, till I call for you in the morning." In a healthy mind there is an interim between one duty and another. This prevents them from wearing each other out. These intervals of soothing carelessness, if not unduly prolonged, are very restorative. Lord Burleigh in the morning resumed his robe of office with zest, because he had been able to throw it off so lightly.

That leisure is compatible with a good deal of work I learned as a child from my Aunt Frances. She was the wife of the village physician. She had twelve children and lived in a large, rambling house which was not planned for saving steps. Yet she was never in a hurry. A peculiar institution of Aunt Frances's house was the *as-you*. It saved no end of worry. When anything was lost, my aunt would say placidly, "You'll probably find it on the as-you"; and so we usually did.

The as-you was a broad landing on the stairs that led from the basement kitchen to the living-room. Usually the members of the family had their hands full when they went upstairs. In such cases they were apt to leave something in the landing with the full assurance that it would be there for them when they made the next trip. The remark that you would find a household article "as you go up," or "as you go down," had been, at last, contracted into a place-name.

I think that every well-ordered mind ought to have an as-you. It is not like an attic where you put decrepit pieces of furniture which you think you will use again, but which you never do.

There are duties which you lay down temporarily because you have your hands too full. You don't want to put them aside where you will forget them. You want to put them where you can pick them up again without too much trouble. There they lie in plain view. You have a feeling that you have carried them as far as you are able to-day. As you come that way to-morrow it will be a pleasure to take them up again. In the meantime they are quite safe on the as-you.

THE LEISURABLE HOURS OF
JOHN WESLEY

LET one who thinks that leisure is beyond the reach of the busy man, and beneath the attention of the man in earnest, read the Journal of John Wesley. It is the record of an intensive religious campaign carried on for more than fifty years with unabated ardor. No Sabbath-breaker was more oblivious to the distinction between the days of the week than Wesley. All days were alike to him. They were all filled with preaching and planning and all sorts of personal services. Five o'clock was the hour for the first sermon, then on horseback or by chaise to speak to a vast multitude in another town, then to horse again, and in the evening a fervent appeal to another great congregation. This was not an occasional outburst of activity; it was Wesley's routine. In all weathers and over all kinds of roads, through Georgia, through Ireland and Wales and Scotland, and through all the English countryside, he was traveling incessantly, greeted at one village by serious-minded Methodists, and at the next by a howling mob. Frequently the two classes mingled.

"It rained incessantly," he says, "as we rode to Grimsby where I preached to a mixed congregation, some of whom were exceeding serious, and some of whom were exceeding drunk."

He apologizes for an off day. "It being a thorough rain, I could only preach at Newgate at eight in the morning and at two in the afternoon, in a house near Hannam Mount at eleven, and in one near Rose-green at five. At the Society in the evening many were cut to the heart."

One would as little look for leisure in such a life as for arbutus on a city street. And, indeed, at the beginning Wesley made no provision for unoccupied time. The very term "Methodist" arose from the methodical division of time adopted by the Holy Club at Oxford. Every moment had its pious exercise and moral task.

On his voyage to Georgia, Wesley followed the self-imposed rule with utter ruthlessness. "We now began to be a little regular. Our common way of living was this. From four in the morning till five, each of us used private prayer. From five to seven, we read the Bible together. At seven we breakfasted. At eight were the public prayers. From nine to twelve I usually learned German, and Mr. Delamotte Greek. My brother writ sermons and Mr. Ingham instructed the children. At twelve we met to give an account to one another of what we had done since our last meeting and what we designed to do before our next." So the day passed on with deadly precision, each hour with its prescribed duty, till "at eight we met again to exhort and instruct one another." At nine they went to bed.

But as he became busier, Wesley became a little irregular in his mental habits, and after a while delightfully so. He filled the interstices of his day with all sorts of irrelevant meditations and observations. He contracted the habit of reading on horseback.

"Near thirty years ago I was thinking, How is it that no horse ever stumbles while I am reading? (History, poetry and philosophy I commonly read on horseback, having other employment at other times.) No account can possibly be given but this, then I throw the reins on his neck. . . . I aver that in riding above a hundred thousand miles, I scarce remember my horse (except two that would fall head over heels anyway) to fall, or make any considerable stumble, while I rode with a slack rein. . . . A slack rein will prevent stumbling if anything will."

He gradually adopted the philosophy of the loose rein in his reading. There seems to have been no particular choice of books. The fervent preacher seemed to have felt no responsibility for the guidance of his thoughts between sermons. That a book was dull was nothing against it. "It is well," he remarks, after perusing such a volume, "that every class of writers has a class of readers." For himself, he liked to mingle with all classes in his off hours.

He reads the works of Bolingbroke, Chesterfield, Voltaire, and Rousseau, and catches no harm, though many a pious convert might have been shocked to see what volumes were in the fervent itinerant's saddle bags. The brief entries show no sense of incongruity.

"I preached about noon at Hanslop, on my way looked over a volume of Swift's letters."

"I went on reading an odd book entitled 'A Chinese Fragment.' "

"Having a leisure hour, I made an end of that strange book, Ariosto's 'Orlando Furioso.' "

He tells how his head was filled with confused

visions of "Astolpho's shield and horn, and the voyage to the moon, the lance that unhorses every one, the all-penetrating sword, and I know not how many impenetrable helmets and coats of mail."

On the whole, he preferred Tasso to Ariosto as a wayside companion. It was a pleasant day when he rode to Chatham reading Tasso's "Jerusalem Delivered," and "in the evening preached to a crowded congregation ready for the promises of God."

"I rode to Epworth and preached in the evening on the third of Jonah. I read to-day part of the 'Meditations' of Marcus Aurelius Antoninus. What a strange Emperor! And what a strange heathen! . . . I make no doubt but that this is one of those 'many' who 'shall come from the east and the west and sit down with Abraham, Isaac and Jacob,' while 'the children of the kingdom,' nominal Christians, are shut out."

"I took another ride to Sundon and on the road read Strada 'De Bello Belgico,' an historian scarce inferior to Livy or Tacitus."

During a busy week in Ireland, he has time to speculate on the veracity of Herodotus, and then to question whether Belisarius was really as badly treated by the Emperor Justinian as some historians aver. These speculations do not prevent him from remarking that the Irish question is still unsettled. "Thence we went on to Belfast through miserable roads. O where is common sense?"

What juxtapositions of thought and feeling we find on every page.

"*Wed.* 19. I preached to my old loving congregation at Osmotherly, and visited once more poor Mr. Watson, just quivering over the grave. I read as I traveled a famous book which I had not looked into for these fifty years. It was Lucian's 'Dialogues.' He has a good deal of humor, wonderful little judgment."

"On going to Dorking I read Mr. Jones's ingenious tract on 'Clean and Unclean Beasts.'" The next day he remarks, "I casually took a volume of what is called 'A Sentimental Journey through France and Italy.' ... In returning I read a very different book published by an honest Quaker on that execrable sum of all villainies, the Slave Trade."

"*Jan.* 1, 1776. About eighteen hundred of us met together in London in order to renew our covenant with God, and it was as usual a very solemn opportunity." The next day: "*Tues.* 2. I set out for Bristol and read over that elegant trifle, 'The Correspondence between Theodosius and Constantia.'" In his "vacant hours" on the following week, he concerned himself "about those greatly injured characters, Richard III and Mary, Queen of Scots." He was aware that in admiring them he might appear singular, but he says, "I must speak as I think, although still waiting for and willing to receive better information."

A "History of Palmyra" he finds less interesting than he hoped for. "On Monday I went down to Bristol again and read on the way Dr. Bride's 'Practice of Physic.' Undoubtedly it is an ingenious book, but it did not answer my expectations." An essay on the "Music of the Ancients" was more rewarding. He takes delight in books he had never heard of before and is inclined, as all discoverers are, to give them exaggerated praise.

"After preaching, I had a very, very pleasant journey to Wheatley, and the next day to London. In this journey I read over that strange book, 'The Life of Sextus Quintus,' an hog driver at first, then a monk, a Bishop, a Cardinal, a Pope. He was certainly as great a genius in his way as any that ever lived."

On the road from Aberdeen to Dundee, he reads the poems of Ossian with great satisfaction. "What a poet was Ossian! What a hero was Fingal!"

"At leisure hours this week I read the 'Life of Sir William Penn,' a wise and good man. But I was much surprised at what he relates of his first wife, who lived, I suppose, fifty years, and said, a little before her death, 'I bless God I never did anything wrong in my life.'" This remark, Wesley said, was quite heathenish.

"In the coach going and coming I read several volumes of Mr. Guthrie's ingenious 'History of Scotland.' I never read any writer before who gave me so much light into the real character of that odd mixture King James the First." He likes Guthrie, too, because he confirms him in his own romantic admiration of Mary, Queen of Scots. However he may have thought about her in his preaching hours, Wesley found Mary altogether adorable as a person to read about. "That much injured Queen," he says, "appears to have been by far the greatest woman of that age, exquisitely beautiful in person, of a fine address, of a deep, unaffected piety, and of a stronger understanding even in youth than Queen Elizabeth had at threescore."

No wonder that Wesley took up the cudgels against John Knox and his fellow reformers who made the fair Queen weep!

"We rode on a mild, cool day to Thorny Hill, about sixty miles from Glasgow. Here I met with Mr. Knox's 'History of the Church of Scotland.' Could any man wonder if the members of it were more fierce, sour, and bitter of spirit than some of them are? For what a pattern they have before them!"

For Ignatius Loyola he had more personal admiration. "I rode to Oxford and next day to Evesham. On Wednesday and Thursday, in riding from Evesham to Bristol, I read over that surprising book, 'The Life of Ignatius Loyola,' surely one of the greatest men that ever supported a bad cause."

Luther he took with a grain of salt. "I finished the translations of Martin Luther's life. Doubtless he was a man highly favored of God and a blessed instrument in his hand. But O what a pity that he had no faithful friend, none that would at all hazards rebuke him plainly and

sharply for his rough, intractable spirit and bitter zeal for opinions so greatly obstructive to the
work of God."

Riding to Canterbury, his mind naturally
turned to Church history. In the open air his
mind moved freely and he perceived, as George
Fox under similar circumstances perceived,
the lamentable limitations of the ecclesiastical
mind. Church history did not read well out of
doors.

"*Monday, August* 5. I set out for Canterbury.
On the way I read Mr. Baxter's 'History of the
Councils.' It is utterly astonishing, and would
be wholly incredible, but that his vouchers are
beyond all exception. What a company of execrable wretches have they been (one cannot give
them justly a milder title) who have in almost
every age since Saint Cyprian taken upon them
to govern the Church! How has one council
been perpetually cursing one another, and deliv-
ering all over to Satan, whether predecessors or
contemporaries, who did not implicitly receive
their determinations, though generally trifling,
sometimes false and frequently unintelligible
or self-contradictory! Surely Mohammedanism
was let loose to reform the Christians! I know

not but that Constantinople has gained by the change."

In his out-of-door readings and meditations, Wesley formed a number of independent opinions about the Mohammedans. A short time before, he was inclined to think that if he had lived in India he would have been happier under the rule of the Great Mogul than under the foreign rule of the East India Company. "The Great Mogul, Emperor of Hindoostan, one of the mightiest potentates on earth, is become a poor, impotent slave to a company of merchants. His large, flourishing empire is broken in pieces, and covered with fraud, oppression, and misery. And we may call the myriads that have been murdered happy in comparison with those who still groan under the iron yoke."

As to the English exploiters of India: "What utter strangers to justice, mercy, and truth, and to every sentiment of humanity! I believe no heathen history contains a parallel. I remember none in the annals of antiquity; not even the divine Cato, or the virtuous Brutus plundered the provinces committed to their charge with such merciless cruelty as the English have plundered the devastated provinces of Hindoostan."

"While in Dublin I read two extraordinary books of different kinds." This seems to have been a frequent device of Wesley. With two extraordinary books of different kinds he was certain to find something interesting going on in his mind.

Crossing to the Isle of Man, he provided himself with Dr. Johnson's "Tour through Scotland," which he enjoyed immensely. He was delighted to find that Johnson was more just to the Scotch than he had been led to expect from the criticisms of the book which he had read. "The calm continuing, I read over Mr. Pennant's 'Tour through Scotland.' How amazingly different from Dr. Johnson's! He is doubtless a man both of sense and learning. Why has he, then, bad English in almost every page? No man should be above writing correctly."

Sometimes his zealous converts do not understand his mental processes. When a prominent Methodist layman objects to his miscellaneous reading, he keeps silence, remarking that he has learned not to contradict a sea captain who is seventy years old. Wesley was then in the eighties.

Sufficient unto the day were the meetings

thereof. In the times between sermons, Wesley gave his mind to the various interests which claimed momentary attention. Each interest had for the time his whole attention.

"About five on Sunday in the evening, I began preaching at Gwennap to full twenty thousand people, and they were so commodiously placed in the calm, still evening that every one heard distinctly." On Tuesday he was engaged in theological controversy, and "the Antinomians gnashed on me with their teeth." The next day he deals with practical morality in his desire "to make the stout-hearted tremble." On Sunday he preaches to another kind of congregation, and remarks, "I wondered at the exquisite stupidity of the hearers."

On Monday morning he arises bright and early with a whole day to meditate on the problems of political economy.

"*Mon.* 2. On my way to Exeter, I read over an ingenious tract containing some observations which I never saw before. In particular, that if corn sells for twice as much now as it did at the time of the Revolution, it is in effect no dearer than it was then, because we have now twice as much money; that if other things now sell for twice as much as they did then, corn ought to do so, too; that though the price of all things increases as money increases, yet they are really no dearer than they were before; and that, lastly, to petition Parliament to alter these things is to put them upon impossibilities and can answer no end but that of inflaming them against their governors."

It was the day after that preaching at Axminster he makes a remark that betrays the humanist: "At five I preached in the market place at Axminster to a still larger congregation. I have seldom heard people speak with more honesty and simplicity than many did at the love feast that followed. I have not seen a more unpolished people than these, but love supplies all defects. It supplies all the essentials of good breeding without the help of a dancing master."

That is an observation that is worthy of the attention of those educators who are concerned about that mysterious thing called "culture," which they often fail to recognize when it appears in a different dress.

For more than half a century we can watch the growth of the mind of John Wesley, in all weathers. His mind became more flexible with age. He found more things to interest him, more different kinds of people with whom he could sympathize. He could enjoy reading the life of Saint Katharine of Genoa, whom he calls "a fool of a saint," and the next hour take up Juvenal. He could read books with great enjoyment without feeling called upon to agree with the author.

Monday 6. "Looking for a book in our college library I took down by mistake the Works of Episcopius; which opening on an account of the Synod of Dort I believed it might be useful to read it through." The next entry is "Being in the Bodleian Library I light on Mr. Calvin's account of the case of Michael Servetus."

"On Friday 26 I took coach and on Saturday reached London. On the journey read Dr. Warner's 'History of Ireland' from its first settlement to the English Conquest. I do not believe one leaf of it is true from beginning to end. I totally reject the authorities on which he builds. I will not take Flaherty's or Keating's word for a farthing. I doubt not Ireland was before the Christian era fully as barbarous as Scotland or England."

If there had been an Irish patriot in the coach as the Methodist preacher laid down the book with this last remark, I am sure he would have shaken hands amicably. Perhaps there was a time when Ireland wasn't so superior to England as the bards would have us believe.

At any rate, the evangelist who went about calling sinners to repentance enjoyed most of all calling Irish sinners to repent, they did it so charmingly. He always mentions the little Irish villages caressingly. "I rode to Bally Shannon, and found an earnest, simple people."

"Instead of going straight to Tullamore, I could not be easy without going round by Cooleylough. I knew not why."

We see him traveling through Ireland with many pleasant interruptions. "With much difficulty I broke away from this immeasurably loving people, and not so soon as I imagined neither, for when we drew near to the turnpike about a mile from the town a multitude awaited us at the top of the hill. They fell back on each side to make way for us and then joined and closed us in. After singing two or three verses I put forward."

Preaching on an Irish village green, Catholics

and Protestants joined in the congregation. One of them, after listening cried, 'Aye, he is a Jesuit, that's plain!' To which a Popish priest who happened to be near replied aloud, 'No! he is not! I wish to God he was!' "

"*May* 18, 1785. On my way to Limerick I read and carefully considered Major Vallance's Irish Grammar, allowed to be the best extant." He grumbles over it as a schoolboy might: "The difficulty of reading it is intolerable, occasioned chiefly by the insufferable number of mute letters both of vowels and consonants, the like of which is not to be found in any language under heaven. The number of pronouns and the irregular formation of the verbs is equally insufferable."

As Wesley was then in his eighty-third year, there was no reason why he should read an Irish Grammar on his way to Limerick. It was certainly from no sense of duty. He had leisure to satisfy an innocent curiosity. He had heard that Irish was a hard language to learn and now he knew it.

"Rode cheerfully to Castlebar." And what a pleasant place to preach in was Rabin in Connaught! "It was an old castle standing between

two loughs with a river behind it and wood before it, and the inhabitants

> "Did like the scene appear,
> Serenely pleasant, calmly fair,
> Soft fell their words as flew the air."

John Wesley the humanist enjoyed preaching in
such a pleasant place to such pleasant people,
while John Wesley the Evangelist was perform-
ing a stern moral duty. Somehow neither of
these personalities interfered with the other.
When we come to think about it, why should
they?

He found Scotland less congenial, but he records his pleasure in preaching in the churchyard at Kelso, and afterwards walking to see the
view from Roxburgh Castle. He would have enjoyed it still more if he had known that there
was among his listeners a little lad, Walter Scott
by name, who afterwards was to add to the romance that surrounds the name of Mary Stuart.

I like to think of the aged John Wesley and
the young Walter Scott face to face. Scott in his
prime loved to pose before his friends as a gentleman of large leisure, while he concealed his hours
of hard work. Wesley would have been remem-
bered only for his prodigious labors if he had not

kept a journal. This reveals the number of delightfully "vacant hours" when he rode with a slack rein and followed the devices of his own heart. It is leisure snatched from the jaws of zeal.

SOME ALLEVIATIONS OF OUR
RESPONSIBILITIES

THE Stoics divided all events into two classes, those for which we are responsible, and those for which we are not responsible. The good man was one who took up the responsibilities that belonged to him and bore them manfully. To the other things that came to pass against his will, he cultivated a wise indifference. They were none of his business, and he refused to disquiet his soul over evils that were inevitable.

This was wholesome teaching. The Christian doctrine was based on the same discrimination. "Cast thy burden on the Lord," says one text. "Let every man bear his own burden," says another. There are things we can change by our action. Let us do our best to direct these things in the right direction. There are laws of nature and facts of the universe which we cannot alter. Here we must trust a higher wisdom than our own. Piety and common sense unite in recognizing these distinctions.

But though the two categories remain, there is

a difference in what we put into them. Actions which once were considered as belonging to the things indifferent are placed under the head of matters for which we are to be held strictly accountable. There is no doubt that, as society grows more advanced, it makes the way of the transgressor harder, and also reveals new transgressions among the well-thought-of. It increases the number of sins, and takes away some of the most venerable excuses.

The reason for this is obvious. It comes from the advance of science which is continually discovering the causes of specific evils and their practical remedies. Science is the great detective. Once on the trail of the evildoer, it spares no dignitaries and accepts no excuses. It is no respecter of persons, and carries its investigations even into the assembly of the saints.

What are the causes of typhoid fever, of cholera, of tuberculosis, of pauperism, of war, of stunted childhood, of arrested mental development, of hideous and cruel social inequalities, of our crowded tenements, and of our cheerless homes?

In the pre-scientific days men cheerfully and innocently pleaded ignorance. We surely do not know, good people said. These things have always been and we must accept them as part of the universe. 'Cast thy burdens on the Lord,' said the religious; 'these things are indifferent,' said the stoical. 'Let us live bravely and cheerfully as if they did not exist. We cannot prevent these evils whose causes we can never know.'

But all agreed that the good man was the one who would do all he could to mitigate the evils he was unable to prevent. When the pestilence walked in darkness, he prayed for the victims and tenderly cared for them, and, when they died, gave them burial. What more could he do?

But all the time men of science have been patiently continuing their investigations. The pestilence no longer is allowed to walk in darkness. The deadly germ is isolated. Its breeding-places are discovered. Its behavior is investigated. Its natural enemies are sought out and put upon its track. At last it is clearly demonstrated that it can be destroyed and its deadly work prevented. The wholesale destruction of life, which men accepted as inevitable, is not inevitable. We, as members of the social order, can do away with it if we are willing to pay the price.

But are we willing to pay the price? And if we are not willing, what kind of persons are we? These are the stern questions which come with every scientific advance. The discovery that an evil is preventable leads immediately to the inquiry, "Are you going to prevent it?"

This enormous increase in our knowledge of preventable evils, while it has stimulated many minds to action, has had on others a paralyzing effect. The evils of all this unintelligible world could be borne. It is the intelligible world that crushes us. We know more than we feel capable of doing. The sense of social and individual responsibility has been preached to us. But how can we keep in a healthy frame of mind while we do what we can to fulfill our manifold obligations? After all, it is more important that we be of sane mind and sound body than that we have spurts of reforming zeal which leave us nervous wrecks.

> "The World Soul knows his own affair,
> Fore-looking when he would prepare
> For the next ages men of mould,
> Well embodied, well ensouled,
> He cools the present's fiery glow
> Sets the life-pulse strong but slow."

For the steady pull we need men and women of

the strong, slow life-pulse. We must not only be conscious of our new responsibilities, but must learn how to bear them buoyantly.

. There are certain suggestions, which come from experience in dealing with difficult situations, which may help in our mental and moral confusion. They may serve to alleviate our too painful sense of responsibility.

One is the simple device of the *elimination of grade crossings* in our minds. Where the highway crosses the railroad, there are warning signs so plain that the wayfaring man, though a fool, cannot err in regard to their meaning. He is urged to "Stop! Look! and Listen!" If there were only one wayfaring man, and only one or two trains a day, this might be sufficient for safety. But, when the traffic has increased and there are hundreds of wayfaring men of limited intelligence, stopping, looking, and listening for trains that are continually thundering by, the condition becomes intolerable. It is not simply that accidents happen to people who take chances, but that the prudent are delayed and their business interrupted. The elimination of grade crossings becomes a necessity.

A large amount of the confusion which we

complain of, and which we attribute to the increasing complexity of modern life, could be obviated by a little attention to traffic management. The trouble is, not that the facts with which we have to deal are various, but that we have only one way of dealing with them. Our purposes are continually coming into collision because they cross each other on a level. Each of these cross-purposes, when considered by itself, is justified. But when we follow one line of thought we unexpectedly meet another line of thought moving at right angles with it. If, at every one of these dangerous grade crossings, we stop, our intellectual progress is slowed up, and we do not use our minds to their full capacity.

By the elimination of these grade crossings, unfortunate accidents may be avoided and a good many thoughts may be kept moving in different directions. This is done by making accurate definitions, and then remembering them after we have made them. This is what a judge does with the intricate cases which are brought before him. It is not sufficient that certain words should be quoted correctly. He asks, What is their meaning "within the statute"?

The same words may mean different things

when used in different connections. The old distinction between good and evil is so fundamental that nobody can get away from it. We speak of a good man, a good play, a good novel, a good intention, a good neighbor, good politics, good art, a good education, a good fight, a good investment. But confusion comes when a good man writes a bad play, and the bad man writes a good one; when good morals are expressed in bad art; when the reformer with the best intentions plays politics poorly; when a good neighbor belongs to the wrong party; and the man with a good education makes a bad mess of the business matters entrusted to his care. In dealing with these combinations, it is hard to keep clear the distinction between good and evil.

If the morally bad, the artistically bad, the economically bad, the hygienically bad always coincided, then it would be an easy matter to be a militant Christian. Having renounced the Devil and all his works, all that would be necessary after that would be to stand fast in our righteous antipathies. But what if the works which we had attributed to the Devil had really been performed by our best friends, or, worse still, if they are performed by ourselves? The story of "Typhoid Mary" is instructive. Persons who themselves may be in good health may yet be the carriers of disease. How many excellent people have been the carriers of baleful superstitions and prejudices? They were the unconscious "hosts" of the evil, just as the innocent currant bush is the host of the micro-organism that causes the blight in the white pine. The mistakes of the saints may be visited on the sinners who follow them.

We cannot use our minds freely and to any advantage, unless we have a good understanding with ourselves as to just what we are trying to get at, and what track we intend to use. It is not a matter of how far we are to go in a certain direction, but of whether the way is clear for us.

Only when we have properly defined the nature of our inquiry do we have the possibility of a direct answer. Which was the greater general, Robert E. Lee or Ulysses S. Grant? This is a question of military science. So long as it is discussed from this standpoint, the discussion is fruitful. But we become confused, and after a time irritated, when irrelevancies, like the right of the States to secede, are introduced. These political questions should have their day in court, but they have no bearing on the issue now presented. Even the question of pacifism must not be allowed to interfere with our interest in military genius. Even if we granted that war is always bad, we might wish to know who carried it on in the most skillful fashion.

The advancement of each special science is dependent on the definition of its scope. Geology is materialistic, though the geologist may be an idealist. Biology knows nothing of the moral law. The truths of physics are not dependent on any theological speculation. Force can be measured and is the same whether devoted to a good end or a bad.

The seeker after truth in any one of these directions must disclaim responsibility for the way in which his discoveries fit into the general scheme of things. For the moment they may seem to produce discord rather than harmony. All that he can say is that he is not responsible for the universe. He only gives a plain answer to a direct question.

That there is an ultimate harmony, and that the result of all honest thinking is a higher unity, is a matter of faith. Any philosophy of life that gives satisfaction is based upon such a belief.

But we can afford to wait for this harmony until the facts to be harmonized are discovered and brought together. In the meantime, it is well to recognize the facts, even though they seem to be most irreconcilable.

The truth-seeker has reason to emulate the adventurous spirit of Stefansson, when he wrote to the naval officials telling them of his plans for two years on the Arctic ice, and ended with the request, "Please do not rescue us prematurely."

Another suggestion as to a help in bearing real responsibilities may be found in the recognition of the principle of *limited liability*. When the stockholder in a company was held liable for its debts to the full extent of his fortune, it was evident that he could not prudently make investments in many large projects, the failure of any one of which would ruin him. When his liability is limited to what he actually puts into any one concern, the sphere of his operations may be with safety enlarged. The vast aggregations of wealth made up of the savings of multitudes of people of small means is characteristic of modern business. The capitalistic system has been democratized and its risks distributed.

It is in vain that we urge a person to be "socially minded," unless we at the same time show him the way to keep himself morally solvent. What obligation does he assume when he joins with others in some undertaking for the common good? We talk of narrow partisanship or narrow sectarianism. We speak scornfully of the parochial type of mind. The narrowness, however, is often only a kind of prudence. A man unites with others whom he knows, and whose sphere of operations lies within the circle of his own observation. He belongs to that group, and feels a personal responsibility for it. All that lies outside of that seems remote and dangerous.

The vast number of organizations each with its special object is very confusing to the person of the parochial intelligence. He imagines that it is possible for him to sympathize and coöperate with only one church, one party, one nation, one social group. He is perplexed by the rival claims made upon his loyalty. He feels responsible, not only for the professed aims of the group to which he belongs, but for the motives and the characters of all his fellow members. The burden of such liability becomes too great for him to bear.

Now the socially minded man moves freely in the modern world because he has come to another idea of group loyalty. He finds it possible to belong to many groups, and to render loyal service to each one in its turn and according to its need.

To what does he belong? When he sits down to count up his interests, he is surprised to find how diversified they are. He is interested in religion, politics, education, business prosperity, philanthropy, art, wholesome amusements, and the advancement of science. There are any number of special interests and activities that appeal to him. These things do not go of themselves. They have to be properly organized and engineered.

Now, it is possible for him to have a share in all these activities if he is only modest enough to recognize that he is only a small shareholder and is expected to contribute only according to his limited means. He may not be on the governing board, or even be recognized by the treasurer as paying annual dues to many institutions which belong to him as a member of the community. He recognizes them all as rendering valuable community service. In case of emergency he relies on them to perform their proper functions. He sleeps better at night because he knows that they are there, just as the soldier sleeps better because he knows that there are sentinels who are doing their duty by not sleeping. He is willing to take his turn when the time comes.

The phrase "one of ours" expresses a regimental loyalty. But the soldier who responds to this feeling is also capable of a larger and even stronger attachment to the army to which the regiment belongs. Coöperation for a common purpose is taken for granted.

This interrelation of the groups that compose a community is very real. Those who appeal to class consciousness forget that each individual belongs to many classes, and as he becomes intelligent he becomes conscious of this fact. For each new ideal which he tries to realize, he seeks sympathy and coöperation. He finds it among the most unexpected people. After working with them for one specific purpose, he cannot think of them as strangers or enemies because on other points they disagree. They are, ever afterwards, potential fellow laborers. He never knows how soon he may need them again.

"How can two walk together except they be agreed?" They can walk together very happily as long as their ways lie together. At the next milestone their ways part, but it is no use to anticipate that divergence. Up to that point they may keep step and enjoy a pleasant conversation. At the fork of the road they separate, but each one is a little nearer to his own goal than when they began to walk together. These free associations bring us in the course of a lifetime into cordial, though often temporary, union with all sorts and conditions of men.

A presidential election is a lesson in tolerance. We stand in front of the newspaper office eager to get the returns. Will our candidate be the next President? Is the paramount issue to be decided in our favor? The Nation is for the moment divided into two classes: those who are with us, and those who are against us. And how catholic we are in our tastes and how broad is our welcome into our party! When we hear of a precinct that on the last election voted for our enemies, and now returns to our fold, we rejoice. There is no carping criticism of motive. Every vote counts, and we need all the help that we can get. When one city and State after another endorse our ticket, we go home filled with satisfaction. The country is saved, and the principles of democracy are again justified. Each one of these millions of unknown voters who were on our side had his own reasons for marking his ballot as he did. Some of these reasons we might not approve, but we do not care for that. We are thinking of the results.

A *rational system of bookkeeping* is a great help. Many persons live under the continued apprehension of moral bankruptcy when they are really quite solvent. Their entries in the debit and credit columns are mixed and give them needless anxiety. Being of a conscientious disposition, they enter everything to be *done* in the column of duties. Being determined to place duty before pleasure, they find the day crowded. The grim-faced duties with eyes fixed on the moral law march past in a drab procession, and the poor little pleasures sit on the curbstone watching for a chance that never comes.

All that may be changed by the simple device of making a pleasure of a duty. The emancipated duty, promoted to the position of a pleasure, leads the procession. The chances are that a lot of dull little duties that had been plodding along forget how dull they are, and act just as if they were pleasures too.

I do not like to explain this on the theory of auto-suggestion which takes for granted that we are playing tricks on our unconscious self. He, poor fellow, has troubles of his own, and it is a pity to make him the dupe of his more intelligent partner. If he is deceived, he has a way of getting his revenge.

What I have in mind is something open and aboveboard. It is simply calling things by their right names, and seeing them as they are. A pleasure is something we enjoy doing. There is no reason why we should not enjoy what is good for us and other people. Incidentally we may be obeying the law of the land.

There is something arbitrary and ungrateful in the way we put a *must* before our privileges, and then take them up as new burdens. Many of the things which we treat as new burdens are only new ways of relieving us of old burdens. Most prohibitions are, when cheerfully accepted, great alleviations of our responsibilities.

I take up a railroad time-table and am confronted with a list of "don'ts":

Don't get off a moving car.

Don't put your hand on the door jamb.

Don't alight from the trains on the wrong side.

Don't walk on the tracks.

Now, if I am in a querulous mood, I resent this intrusive didacticism on the part of the public service corporation. Must I keep all these things in mind every time I take a little journey in the world? But when I am in a more reasonable frame of mind, I realize that these are not things I am required to do. They refer to what I am not in the habit of doing and they commend me. The railroad company is simply patting me on the back and praising me for not getting off a moving car and not putting my hand on the door jamb. These abstentions have become so easy that they have long since ceased to be a burden. Because I have given heed to these "don'ts" I am still alive. That the railroad company should call attention to this happy circumstance is not a cause for irritation, but for hearty congratulations.

That is the way we should look at social legislation devised for our benefit. It is the rational way of looking at labor-saving inventions. Why should we not take them in the spirit in which they are offered? If they do not save labor, but only increase it, whose fault is it?

To come back to the teaching of the Stoics, there is one thing for which we must assume responsibility, and that is the government of our own minds. A man must be master in his own house. The more he is able to rule himself, the more easily he can do his necessary work in the world. What kind of government should he establish in the interest of his own peace? This will be considered in the next essay.

SUGGESTIONS FOR
THE ESTABLISHMENT OF
A CONSTITUTIONAL GOVERNMENT
IN ONE'S OWN MIND

MR. BRYAN, in the days when he was a progressive politician instead of a perturbed theologian, used to say that the paramount issue in this campaign is, Who shall rule? Mr. Bryan was right. A nation may have among its citizens thousands of honest, intelligent, and refined persons who for all political purposes may be negligible. With all their personal virtues, they may be unable to make their will effective.

The same thing is true in regard to a person who is recommended for a position of responsibility. We ask, "What kind of a mind has he?" But, after all, the more important question is, "How does he govern the mind that he happens to have?" Out of the mob of instincts, aptitudes, motives, talents, and inhibitions, how is anything decided? What is the power which rules? It is only with that dominating and decisive element that we can do business.

The Hebrew sage declared that he that ruleth his own spirit is greater than he that taketh a city. This is literally true. Many persons who have made a great stir in the world have made woeful failures in the government of their own minds. They have never overcome their native anarchy. The difficulty is not so much in original endowment as in the lack of governmental arrangements. While we recognize the enormous complexity of the world of politics, we conceive of what takes place within us with too great simplicity. We do not keep up with modern progress in the science of government.

The mediæval ballad says, "My mind to me a kingdom is." That was taken quite literally. The mind was conceived of as an absolute monarchy, and not as a republic, with a government of laws. One ruling principle was acknowledged, and all that was opposed to that was kept in strictest subjection.

The person with an autocratically governed mind is free from many disturbing doubts. He has only one ruling idea at a time. He decides between This and That; he does not allow This to be moderated by That. Every thought has a certain absoluteness and finality about it.

The working of the autocratic mind is seen in the story of Esther. Haman comes to King Ahasuerus and suggests that it would be a good thing on a certain day to kill all the Jews in Persia. The King is struck favorably by the thought, and without more ado sends messengers on horses and swift dromedaries, with orders for the pogrom. Then Queen Esther comes and pleads the cause of her people. But the theory of absolute autocracy leaves no room for vacillation on the part of the monarch. The decree has been sent out, and the law of the Medes and the Persians cannot be changed. But, of course, the King can issue another decree to another set of people. So he sends out messengers on horses and swift dromedaries to all the Jews in his dominions, urging them to rise and slay their adversaries. When the day of glorious slaughter takes place, the King has the satisfaction of knowing that his will has been obeyed by all parties.

According to the Book of Daniel, King Darius was less fortunate when in the same predicament. Having issued his decree, he longed to change it, but he could not; "then the King was sore displeased with himself, and set his heart on Daniel to deliver him." But this was impossible under his system of government, and Daniel had to trust to the magnanimity of the lions for his rescue.

We have all known minds of this nature. They cannot change. They are firm, self-assured, and incapable of compromise. No principle is ever surrendered. There is no deviation from the strictest logic. No half-truth is ever admitted as a half-truth. It must always assert its claim to be the whole truth — *pro tempore*. If two half-truths meet each other, they must not combine; that would be a conspiracy for the restraint of clear thinking. One must kill the other. If both should be destroyed, that would be a still greater simplification of thought. That which remains after *This* and *That* have been eliminated is Neither. If they had been allowed to exist in the mind together, that which remained would have been Both. That is what the autocratic mind cannot tolerate.

That is a disconcerting moment in the political history of your mind when there comes evidence of insurgency against autocratic rule. There is a growing doubt as to whether cocksureness is the test of truth. You discover impulses, ideas, points of view which have been denied expression because they do not agree with the decrees of the ruling powers. But now they clamor for representation. There is a demand for a more democratic control of the mental machinery.

You are in a mood for a Declaration of Independence, and you repeat the fine phrases about the "course of human events" and government by the consent of the governed. Your George the Third may be a theological dogma, or a social convention, or a family tradition, or an imperious fashion, but, whatever it is, you feel that its arbitrary sway should be sharply challenged. Your several faculties which have heretofore been kept in subjection are, and ought to be, free and independent states of mind.

But it is one thing to make a Declaration of Independence, and it is another thing to form a constitution under which we may have a free representation of all the elements in our mental body politic and yet be able to carry on business with reasonable efficiency. Those who seriously undertake the task will find that they come upon all the problems of government which confront the statesman. Nations which attempt to escape autocratic control often fall under the tyranny of a plutocracy, or are caught in the meshes of a bureaucracy, or fall victims to the dictatorship of the proletariat. And so do individuals.

A plutocracy is a government in which accumulated wealth has undue influence. One comes across minds that are governed in this manner The person has accumulations of knowledge that are in excess of his present mental energy. His acquisitions interfere with his judgment. When any new question arises, his regard for vested interests determines his judgment. I have this feeling in regard to such a simple matter as the reform of English spelling. I should not wish to discourage the reformers too much, and yet I should not wish them to be completely victorious in my day. The reason is that I have a certain vested interest in the old-fashioned spelling book. My facility in spelling is not great, but such as it is, it was bought at a price. A leveling process by which people may spell without effort deprives my hard-won accumulations of much of their comparative value. Few people like to relinquish any superiority that has cost them something.

The bureaucratic mind is equally common.

It is a mind where everything is in its place, each fact is in its appropriate cubby-hole. All the intellectual motions go on with automatic precision. Every detail is scrupulously correct. In a bureaucracy every one does his duty as he understands it, and nobody tries to understand any more of his duty than is strictly necessary to his own comfort. Nobody knows what it is all about because it's nobody's business to know. A mind of this kind has a great deal of specialized skill, but it has no general ideas. Everything is looked after except the whole.

The problem of government here is one of co-ordination. The bureaucratic mind prides itself on balancing one consideration against another, without ever doing anything so crude as coming to a big decision. In stating the different aspects of a complicated case, it feels that it has done its full duty. It never brings anything to pass. When one has a large amount of learning at his disposal, this is very imposing. But, after all, a very simple matter may be sophisticated in this way by one who is content to remain in a state of intellectual anarchy.

Says Corin in "As You Like It," "And how like you the shepherd's life, Master Touchstone?" Touchstone answers, "Truly, shepherd, in respect to itself, it is a good life; but in respect that it is a shepherd's life, it is naught. In respect that it is solitary, I like it very well; but in respect that it is private, it is a vile life. Now, in respect that it is in the fields, it pleaseth me well; but in respect that it is not at court, it is tedious. As it is a spare life, look you, it fits my humor, but as there is no more plenty in it, it goes much against my stomach."

I have read books of philosophy which went on in this undulating way chapter after chapter. I said this is what Touchstone would have done if he had had a good education.

A bureaucracy is anarchy disguised as order. The bureaucratic mind does not do things systematically. It delights to systematize the things that are never done.

To bring the various powers of the mind under democratic control and to reconcile the demands of freedom and efficiency, there must be continuous experimentation. The principle of the right of the majority to rule must be established. This means that in a practical decision it is not necessary that all the arguments be on one side. It is sufficient for action if the preponderance of probabilities is clear. The person who acts only on absolute certainties is always too late. But while the majority should rule, the minorities have rights that must be safeguarded. The way must be open to them to become the majority if new evidence is produced. In a free mind, as in a free state, there is no final settlement.

The first amendment to the Constitution of the United States provides a peaceable way for revolutions in thought: Congress shall pass "no law abridging the freedom of speech, or of the press, or the right of the people peaceably to assemble, and to petition the Government for a redress of grievances." According to the Constitution the agitator has rights that must be respected by the legislator. Many persons who pride themselves on their well-ordered minds never get this point of view. When they settle a thing, they want it to stay settled. They will have no soap-box orators obstructing their mental sidewalks and airing their grievances. The opposition must be crushed. Such persons have no doubts and difficulties and their nerves are saved from wear and tear. Their minds are usually well preserved. All we can say is that they are uninteresting.

An interesting mind has doubts, beliefs, purposes, insurgencies, problems, causes, antipathies,
premonitions, tastes, and stern moral principles
— and all of them are alive at the same time.
All the things that are in the actual world are allowed to enter the mind, and there is no alien or
sedition law to prevent their free expression.
But in an interesting mind these elements are
not simply tumbling about in a mental chaos.
Chaos is no more interesting than is an artificial
order which is produced by the elimination of
all complicating elements. What we want is an
active mind that through conflict has come to
some sort of unity with itself.

The governmental problems which arise in
one's mind are very much the same as those
which perplex the makers of constitutions.
How far may the executive, legislative, and
judicial functions be divided? Some minds accept the formal division of our American Constitution. Others prefer the more flexible par-
liamentary system.

You will find many conscientious persons
who suffer from government by injunction. So
many acts are forbidden by arbitrary decree of
the conscience that free play of reason is pre-

vented. They are the victims of their inhibitions.

A great many difficulties in the government of the mind arise when we try to establish a standard of values. It is a matter that has worried constructive statesmen. "Congress," says the first article of the Constitution of the United States, "shall have power to lay and collect taxes, duties, imposts and excises, and to pay the debts of the United States." It also has power to "coin money, regulate the value thereof and of foreign coin."

This is a great power, but in the attempt to exercise it Congress has often got beyond its depth. The attempt to regulate the value of money has led to many hazardous experiments. Nothing is more troublesome than a circulating medium which will not circulate.

Language is to thought what money is to wealth. It is a necessity in the exchange of ideas. It is in our power to multiply words without increasing our intellectual wealth. The result of such inflation is to lower the value of the verbal currency. The inflationist usually meets this crisis by a new emission, and so the vicious circle is completed. As long as we are dealing only with ourselves, this process can be kept up, as our words are made legal tender for domestic debts. It is when we deal with other minds that the question of foreign exchange troubles us. Have you never gone into a committee meeting with a set of valuable phrases, just issued? They were fresh and crisp and crackly like so many new greenbacks. But when you tried to pass them at their face value, you found that they were not received. In order to do any intellectual trading with your neighbors, you must get rid of the delusion of fiat money. There must be something behind your words if they are to be taken at par.

One would avoid, if possible, such a ticklish subject as the tariff, on which one can expect no general agreement. But one cannot deal with the problems of our little republic without coming upon the question of the protection of the infant industry of thinking. It is all very well to say, "We will do our own thinking." But can we afford to when there are so many people with more adequate facilities who are eager to do our thinking for us? There is not a single subject on which we cannot get ready-made opinions in all the standard sizes, cheaper than we can make them ourselves. The finished products of foreign intellects are dumped on our home market, while our own intellectual faculties are suffering from unemployment.

Of course the free-trader answers that all this is in the order of nature, and that we should grin and bear it. Why should we waste our time in thinking when we can get better thoughts furnished by experts at much less cost per thought?

Still, there are those who are incapable of such a detached view, and who try to give their own working classes a certain degree of protection. I have known such a person to lay down a book before he had read ten pages in it. The only excuse that he had was that it set him thinking. He got to thinking on the subject so industriously that he forgot to look further into the volume to see how the author came out. Indeed, his theory was that books were only vessels in which he imported raw materials for his own workshops. I do not know whether this policy can be fully justified, but at least this can be said about it, that, though he never attained to erudition, he at least kept his mind busy.

I suppose that there is no phrase that has afforded more food for thought to the justices of

the Supreme Court than "due process of law."
No person can be deprived of "life, liberty, or
property, without due process of law." When
the Fourteenth Amendment was enacted, it was
not understood how important this phrase was
to become.

Some such conservative provision is needed in
the government of the mind. There is certain intellectual property which we inherit or acquire.
It is possible that in the march of improvement
we may lose it. But, after all, it is ours and we
are attached to it, and wish to preserve it if
possible. There are iconoclasts who have no
respect for such possessions, and would ruth-
lessly sweep them away without thought for
any old associations. I think that in a well-
formed government there should be a certain
amount of legal delay in making radical changes.
Let no person be deprived of a cherished opinion — except by due process of law.

Another phrase which has received about
equal judicial attention is, "Commerce between
the States." Many otherwise excellent minds
suffer because of lack of any system of internal
communications. One idea never suggests another. The isolated thoughts have no means of

getting together. The result is a general impression of dullness. A good-roads movement is demanded. It would result in a development of natural resources and stimulate mental activity. This falls within the province of the general government.

There is a fine suggestion of this in the eighty-fourth psalm. The psalm begins with a note of homesickness. The exiled patriot longs for his dear native land and temple where his fathers worshiped. He envies the sparrow that had found a house and the swallow a nesting-place by the holy altars. Then suddenly the poet changes from homesickness to self-reliance. After all, he says, the difficulty to be overcome is in the mind itself. "Blessed is the man whose strength is in thee, in whose heart are the high ways to Zion."

That direct highway running through the mind may be thronged with eager thoughts. In the opening up of such highways there is the possibility of new prosperity. These internal improvements change the whole situation.

In a constitutionally governed mind the attention is often confined to domestic problems to the neglect of foreign relations. This is manifest in the scornful way in which independent young persons often speak of what they term "mere conventionalities." They do not realize what an important part conventionality plays.

The independent nation is not alone in the world, and it cannot do what it pleases without regard to other equally independent nations. Its relation to these foreign powers is governed by a large number of conventions. These treaties represent the peaceful solution of a vast number of problems. They are the things agreed upon by the high contracting powers. They cannot be abrogated lightly. Infinite confusion would be the result if nations were free from these self-imposed limitations to their free action. Treaty rights are insisted upon as a condition of peace.

Precisely the same thing occurs in the case of the individual in his relations with other members of the community. A state of things where every man does what is right in his own eyes, without any regard to what is expected of him, is a condition of anarchy. A man's thought may be free, but his conduct must be largely determined by the conventions of the community in which he lives. They do not represent ultimate and unchangeable moral laws; they represent the methods agreed upon. When they are changed, it must be by common consent, and after proper diplomatic preparation has been made. The conflicts that arise between what a man, as an individual, prefers, and what is required of him as a member of a highly organized society, cannot be avoided. It is, however, possible to be prepared for them when they come. There is something amiss when we say of a person that he is highly intelligent, high-minded, and conscientious, but somehow he never is able to get on with other people. Before we put all the blame on the other people, we ought to look into the conduct of his foreign office. Perhaps it is a case of too much "shirt-sleeves diplomacy."

SATAN AMONG THE BIOGRAPHERS

By Satan I do not mean the evil spirit who goes about like a roaring lion. I have in mind the Satan who appears in the prologue to the Book of Job. He is the adversary, the one who presents the other side. When the sons of God came together, then came the adversary among them. He belonged to the assembly, but he sat on the opposition bench. He introduced questions which had occurred to him as he walked up and down upon the earth. His function was to challenge generally received opinions. There was Job. Every one looked upon him as a man who was as righteous as he was prosperous. But was he? Satan suggested that his character should be analyzed. Take away Job's prosperity and let us see what becomes of his righteousness.

Now, that critical spirit has entered into the biographers and influenced their attitude toward what they used to call the subject of their sketch. It used to be taken for granted that the tone of biography should be eulogistic. "Let us praise famous men and the fathers who begat us."

This indicates how closely biography is related to genealogy. The text is often transformed into "Let us praise the fathers who begat us, and if we have sufficient literary skill we may make them famous."

The lives of the saints have a great sameness, for it is necessary that they should be saintly. Even when their adventures are of the most astonishing character, the chronicler must throw in a word now and then to show that they are not acting out of character. Thus that wild Irish saint, Saint Brandan, who went careering over the Western Sea like another Sindbad the Sailor, must have a religious motive for his voyage. The chronicler declares, "seven years on the back of a whale he rode, which was a difficult mode of piety." Had Brandan been a layman, we might have admired him for his acrobatic gifts. Being a saint, we must see him balancing himself on the back of a whale as a pious exercise.

Biographers on the whole have been a rather modest folk and have had scant recognition in academic circles. Thus there are numberless professors of history — ancient and modern — but when recently a Minnesota college established a

professorship of biography, the title seemed a
strange one. The educational world has followed
the example of Nature — so careful of the type,
so careless of the single life.

But a new school of biography has arisen, and
it is of interest to compare it with the old. The
great difference is in the attitude of the biographer toward his subject. The attitude of the old
biographer was that of a painter who was com-
missioned to paint the portrait of a great man.
He wished to make a likeness and to make it as
lifelike as possible; but he had to recognize the
proprieties. The painter is frankly on the outside, and can give only so much of character as is
revealed in the countenance. So the biographer
was dealing frankly with externals. What the
great man did or said could be recorded, but
what he meant could only be guessed. Every
man's mind was his castle, and there were private rooms into which the public had no right
to intrude. If a person were very inquisitive, he
might, if he got the chance, peep in through the
windows of the soul; but that was as far as he
could go. He was necessarily an outsider.

But of late the biographer has become bolder
and, instead of peeping in, has taken to breaking

and entering. His method is described as "penetrating." We see him not only prowling in the consciousness, but penetrating into the most remote portions of the subconsciousness. We see him throwing his flashlight upon motives concealed from nearest friends. It is the era of the X-ray, and human character cannot escape the methods of research. The biographer attempts to show us a man's mind as viewed from the inside. How he gets inside is his business — not ours.

Let us compare John Morley's "Gladstone" with Mr. Strachey's "Queen Victoria." Morley takes his subject very seriously. Gladstone was a great man, and knew it, and so did every one else. He lived in a great period and was an important part of it. Morley was a friend who followed his career with respectful but discriminating interest. He was in a position to know a great many facts. But he did not intrude. A vast number of details are given, but the result of it all is that we feel that we are looking *at* Gladstone and not through him. We know what he did and what he said, and we know what interpretations his friend Morley put upon his words and actions; but we can only guess at his ulterior motives. We see the conclusions to which he came, but not all the mental processes by which they were reached. Mr. Gladstone always appears to us clothed and in his right mind. If he had any unlucid intervals, they are not a part of the record. As for exploring Gladstone's subconscious mind, his friend would as soon have thought of poking about in his host's pantry without asking leave. What did Gladstone think when he wasn't addressing the public or preparing to address it? The biographer would say, "That is none of your business, nor is it mine."

The same impression is made by Trevelyan's "John Bright." We feel that we know John Bright as well as his constituents knew him. It never occurs to us that we know him better.

Turn to Mr. Strachey's delightful biography of Queen Victoria. We have a surprise. We are conscious of a new sensation. To say that the book is stimulating is faint praise. It is intoxicating. Here is biography with its crudenesses and irrelevancies distilled away. We get the essential spirit.

It is not that we are behind the scenes as an ordinary playgoer who is allowed this novel experience, that he may see how things look on that side of the curtain. We are behind the scenes as a playwright who is also his own stage manager may be behind the scenes. We feel that somehow we have an intimate knowledge of how the lights should be arranged to produce the best effects. We have no illusions ourselves, but this allows us to watch the production of the play with keener intellectual interest.

We see Queen Victoria, not as her admiring subjects, with superstitious ideas about royalty, saw her, but as she would have seen herself, had she been as clever as we are. The revelation has all the charm that an autobiography would have if a person would speak about himself without vanity and without self-consciousness.

In reading the "Confessions" of Saint Augustine or Rousseau, we feel that they are trying to tell the whole truth about themselves, but we are not convinced that they have succeeded. They confess certain sins that attract their attention; but what of those failings which Saint Paul describes as "the sins that so easily beset us"? Some of these beset a person so closely that he doesn't know that they are there. There are certain commonplace faults which are seldom confessed by the most conscientious. I have never come across an autobiography in which the writer drew attention to the fact that his friends often found him a little wearing.

Mr. Strachey gives us Victoria's autobiography written by somebody else who saw through her. There is an awareness of all her limitations and a cool appreciation of her middle-class virtues. We sympathize with her efforts to live up to her station in life. We see her successes and admire her pluck. When she makes mistakes, we recognize that she is thoroughly conscientious. Her judgments are often shrewd. She is rather muddle-headed in regard to the new problems of the day, but not more so than her constitutional advisers. She is a real character, and we know her in the same way that we know Becky Sharp and Mrs. Proudie. We feel that we not only know what she did, but we know the moving why she did it. We know also why she did not do more. It was because it wasn't in her to do more. And her environment was exactly fitted to her personality. We feel that it was no mere coincidence that she lived in the Victorian Age.

In "Eminent Victorians," Mr. Strachey reversed the methods practiced by writers like

Walter Scott. They took some well-known historical character and allowed their imagination to play about it. The result was Historical Romance, or Romance founded on fact.

Mr. Strachey takes well-known historical characters of the last generation, like Arnold of Rugby, Cardinal Manning, Chinese Gordon, and Florence Nightingale, and shows us that they have become in a short time little better than noted names of fiction. Every man is his own myth-maker and his friends and enemies collaborate in producing something quite different from the reality. The ordinary biography is, therefore, little more than a collection of facts founded on a fiction. The problem, then, is not simply to reëxamine the facts, but to rearrange them so that they will tell a true story and not a false. The biographer is like a typesetter. He must first distribute the type and then set it up again to form new words and sentences.

No saint in the calendar had a legend more firmly fixed and authenticated than Florence Nightingale. The public not only knew what she did, but was convinced that it knew what kind of a person she was. She was the lady with the lamp, the gentle ministering angel who went

about through the hospitals in the Crimea. She
was the one who brought the feminine touch
to war.

Mr. Strachey does not change the outlines of
her story. That is a matter of historic record.
She did all and more than we have been taught
to believe. But he shows Florence Nightingale
as an altogether different kind of a person.

The feminine gives way to a masterful personality. Florence Nightingale was the stuff that
successful politicians and captains of industry
are made of. She appears as a formidable person, abrupt in manner, often bitter in speech, the
terror of evildoers, and still more the terror of
incompetent welldoers. She was strong-minded,
neurasthenic, intense in her antipathies, and
not pleasant to live with; but she got things
done.

She was born in a wealthy family. She wanted
to have her own way, but was never quite sure
what it was to be. This was an endless trouble to
her family, who never knew what to do with
Florence, or rather what Florence would let
them do for her.

When marriage was suggested, she writes:
"The thoughts and feelings I have now I can re-

member since I was six years old. A profession, a trade, a necessary occupation, something to fill and employ all my faculties I have always felt essential to me. Everything has been tried — foreign travel, kind friends, everything. My God, what is to become of me?"

Then came the Crimean War with the breakdown of the hospital service. At last she had her own way, and it proved a gloriously right way. She won immortal fame.

The war ended, and Florence Nightingale had fifty years of invalidism. But she was the same energetic, pugnacious personality. Almost to the end she refused to wear the halo prepared for her by the public which she continued to serve faithfully and acrimoniously. We are made to feel that Florence Nightingale loved her fellow men, but not as an amiable person loves those friends whom he finds congenial. She loved mankind as a thoroughly conscientious person might love his enemies. "Sometimes," says Mr. Strachey, "her rages were terrible. The intolerable futility of mankind obsessed her, and she gnashed her teeth at it."

This is a triumph of biographical reconstruction. We see Florence Nightingale as great and

good, though with a very different assortment
of virtues.

Yet, after all, Mr. Strachey gives us no facts
which Sir Edward Cook had not narrated in his
two-volume biography of Florence Nightingale.
The only difference is that Sir Edward obscures
the significance of many of the facts by his uni-
formly eulogistic comments. Thus he doesn't
say that Florence in her girlhood must have been
a difficult person to live with, but he says: "The
companionship which Florence had at home
was sometimes wearisome to her.... Mamma,
we may suppose was busy with housekeeping
cares. Papa was fond of reading aloud, and in
order to interest his daughters would take them
through the whole of the 'Times' with many a
comment, no doubt, by the way. 'Now for
Parthe,' Miss Nightingale used to say, 'the
morning's reading did not matter; she went on
with her drawing; but for one, who had no such
cover, the thing was boring to desperation. To
be read aloud to is the most miserable exercise of
the human intellect. Or rather is it any exercise
at all? It is like lying on one's back with one's
hands tied, and having liquid poured down one's
throat. Worse than that, because suffocation

would immediately ensue, and put a stop to the operation. But no suffocation would stop the other.'"

The comment of Sir Edward on these revelations of the domestic side of his heroine is in the style of the old biography: "Florence was an affectionate and dutiful daughter. She obeyed and yielded for many years. She strove hard to think that her duty lay at home, and that the trivial round and common task would furnish all that she had any right before God or man to ask." There is something refreshing in Mr. Strachey's judgment on the facts. Florence Nightingale was not a very affectionate daughter or sister, but she was a glorious benefactor to suffering humanity.

When I turn to Arnold of Rugby and Chinese Gordon, I begin to have misgivings. Mr. Strachey's portraits are marvelously clear, but there is something lacking. Looking through the eyes of Thomas Hughes and Dean Stanley, we see Dr. Arnold as a great man. We cannot expect Mr. Strachey to share their awe, for Dr. Arnold was not his schoolmaster. But we do not feel that he accounts for the impression the Doctor made on those who knew him.

As for General Gordon, we see him not through the eyes of a hero worshiper, but as he appeared to one who had no sympathy with his enthusiasms. That irony which is delightful when playing around the figure of Queen Victoria seems out of place when directed toward the hero of Khartum. There was a touch of fanaticism about Gordon, just as there was about Cromwell. But Carlyle's Cromwell stands out against the background of eternity, and is justified. Strachey's Gordon stands condemned against a bleak background of common sense. Even the final tragedy is told without any relenting admiration. The whole thing was so unnecessary. When all was over, we are told of the group of Arabs whom Slatin Pasha saw, one of whom was carrying something wrapped in a cloth. "Then the cloth was lifted and he saw before him Gordon's head. The trophy was taken to the Mahdi; at last the two fanatics met face to face."

Thirteen years after, Kitchener fearfully avenged his death at Omdurman, "after which it was thought proper that a religious ceremony in honor of Gordon should be held at the Palace in Khartum. The service was conducted by four chaplains and concluded with a performance of 'Abide with Me,' General Gordon's favorite hymn. General Gordon, fluttering in some remote Nirvana the pages of a phantasmal Bible, might have ventured a satirical remark. But General Gordon had always been a contradictious person, even a little off his head, perhaps — though a hero; and, besides, he was no longer there to contradict. At any rate, all ended happily in a glorious slaughter of twenty thousand Arabs, a vast addition to the British Empire, and a step in the peerage for Sir Evelyn Baring."

What is it that offends in this? It is the unfairness, not to Gordon, but to his contemporaries. Gordon represented an ideal that belonged to his generation. It was British imperialism touched with a sense of responsibility for the government of the world. We have broken with imperialism, but we ought to be touched by the heroism. In brushing aside the judgment of his contemporaries with a touch of scorn, we feel the kind of unfairness of which Cato complained when, after he had passed his eightieth year, he was compelled to defend himself in the Senate. "It is hard," he said, "to have lived with one generation, and to be tried by another."

Each generation takes itself seriously. It has its own ideals and its own standards of judgment. One who has made a great place for himself in the hearts of his contemporaries cannot be dismissed lightly because he does not conform to the standards of another period. The visitor to Colorado is taken by his friends for a drive over the high plains in sight of the mountains. Pointing to a slight rise of ground that is little more than a hillock, the Coloradan remarks: "That we call Mount Washington, as it happens to be the exact height of your New Hampshire hill."

The New-Englander recalls, with shame at his provincialism, the time when he thought Mount Washington sublime. When he recovers his self-respect, he remembers that a mountain is as high as it looks. It should be measured, not from the level of the sea, but from the level of its surrounding country. Mount Washington seen from the Glen looks higher than Pike's Peak seen from the window of a Pullman car.

In like manner a great man is one who towers above the level of his own times. He dominates the human situation as the great mountain dominates the landscape of which it is a part.

A very alluring opportunity is offered for the scientific study of personages who have made a great place for themselves in history. They have all of them been more or less ailing, and have had "symptoms" of one kind and another. An American medical man has given us a number of volumes entitled "Biographic Clinics."

Mr. Frederick Chamberlin has given us a large volume on "The Private Character of Queen Elizabeth." Elizabeth is defended against the charges made by her enemies, but the defense is damaging to the romance which has gathered around her name. She is treated as if she were an out-patient in the General Hospital. The first thing, of course, is to take her family history. Then we have sixty pages of the medical history of Elizabeth Tudor.

The writer is most conscientious, and says: "Items are numbered consecutively, accompanied by Elizabeth's age and the date of each. It is attempted to confine each disease or illness to one group." In her long life she had a number of ailments. We are spared not one detail. Following the itemized health record, there are twenty-five pages of "The Opinions of Medical Experts." Mr. Chamberlin, who is not by profession a medical man, presented the data he had collected to the leading consultants, to get their opinion as to what was the matter with Queen Elizabeth.

Sir William Osler was rather brief in his answers to the questions. While agreeing that, judging from the records, the patient could hardly be said to be in good health, he says, "Apart from the dropsy, which may have been nephritis, and the smallpox, the descriptions are too indefinite to base any opinion of much value." To Question IV — What was her probable health during the years for which there are no data supplied? — Dr. Osler answers, "Impossible to say."

Sir Clifford Allbutt is equally unsatisfactory. "Would it be too much to say that after her fifteenth year she was practically an invalid with the possible exception of the years for which no data are supplied, directly or indirectly?" He answers, "It would be too much."

But Dr. Keith of the Royal College of Surgeons gives an opinion at great length, accompanied by a clinical chart. We learn that she had anæmia, stomach and liver derangements, septic conditions of the teeth, and the pain in her left arm may have been from rheumatism.

The reader's apprehensions, however, are somewhat relieved by the consideration that all these ailments did not come at once but were scattered over a period of sixty-nine years. Dr. Keith adds very justly that the diagnosis would be more complete had the physician had an opportunity personally to examine the patient. "In the case of Queen Elizabeth, the modern physician is separated from his patient by more than three hundred years; he has to attempt a diagnosis on historical data."

By the way, it is interesting to see how the course of history modifies scientific opinion. When she was about eighteen, Elizabeth had an illness which Dr. Howard at first diagnosed as the most extreme form of kidney disease. "But," he adds, "it seems hardly possible that the subject of nephritis of so severe a type would live to be nearly seventy." He therefore inclines to the theory that the trouble was "acute endocarditis and mitral regurgitation"; and then he adds, with the fairness characteristic of a scientific man, "The same objection to longevity might be raised to this diagnosis also."

Modern pathology may throw light on some historical characters, but one feels that it has its limitations. Not only do the modern physicians find it difficult to make a complete diagnosis when the patient has been dead for three hundred years, but they find it difficult to keep to the highest standard of professional ethics when speaking of the practitioners of a former day.

Thus Sir Clifford, speaking of the doctors who treated Queen Elizabeth, says: "My impression is that in the sixteenth century medicine was below contempt: In Queen Elizabeth's time Clowes did somewhat, and, possibly, Lowe; but really all the medicine of value was in Italy; and only by studying in Italy could our doctors then have known anything. Some few did, of course. The rest were hard-shell Galenists and quacks."

This is rather hard, coming from a consultant of the twentieth century who was called into a case that belonged to medical men of the sixteenth century. The fact that these medical men had kept the patient alive for almost seventy years, while the modern diagnosticians would have given her up at twenty, ought to count for something.

I am willing to admit that pathological inquiries may have their uses for the biographer, but there are limits. In this sphere pathology may be a good servant, but it is a bad master. The same may be said of psychology. The psychologist in his own sphere is a modest and hardworking person. The advancement of any science within its own territory is always slow work. If one is to get results he must work for them and share them with others.

But there is a border line between the sciences which is a fair field for adventure. The bold borderer, with a few merry men, may make a foray and return with booty. The psychiatrists and psychoanalysts have invaded the field of biography in force and are now engaged in consolidating their conquests. Biography is a particularly inviting field. To psychoanalyze a living person takes a great deal of time and patience. But to psychoanalyze historical personages and to point out their various complexes and repressions and conflicts is an inviting pastime. There is no one to contradict.

The old-time theologians in discussing predestination ventured into the recesses of the Divine Mind. Assuming that God both foreknew and foreordained man's fall, they asked which had the priority, foreknowledge or foreordination. Did God foreknow that man would fall and therefore foreordain that he should be punished everlastingly? So said the sub-lapsarians. With more rigid logic the supra-lapsarians contended that foreordination is absolute and independent of all contingencies. God foreordained man's creation, his fall, and his punishment in one decree, and of course he foreknew that the decree would be fulfilled.

Theologians to-day are more modest and are inclined to admit that there are some things which they do not know. But there are biographers whose minds seem to be built on the high supra-lapsarian plan. When we open the book we feel that everything is foreordained. There are no contingencies. The man's character being determined, the biographer presents us with the incidents which illustrate it. We know the kind of a person he is, and his deeds are predetermined.

The clear-cut character sketches in which a man represents a single trait are interesting, but they are most sharply defined when we know ouly one incident. Some of the most familiar characters of the Bible are known only from a chance word or mere gesture. "Gallio cared for none of these things." Generations of preachers have held up Gallio as an example of the sin of indifference. He was the kind of man who, if he lived now, would neglect his religious privileges and forget to register at the primaries. But was Gallio that kind of a man? All we know about this Roman magistrate is that he dismissed a case over which he had no jurisdiction, and in regard to which he had little interest. Had we a glimpse of him on another day, we might revise our opinion.

The name of Ananias has been used as a synonym for habitual liar. But in the Book of the Acts it is not said that Ananias *told* a lie: all that is said is that he sold his possessions and laid part of the price at the Apostle's feet. In other words, Ananias did not, on this occasion, make a complete return of his personal property.

When we remember Lot's wife we have a very clear impression of her character. She was a typical reactionary. And yet all we know about her is that on one occasion she looked back. Had we a complete biography we might learn that on other occasions she had been quite progressive.

When this method is applied to persons whose lives are well known, there will always be a great deal of skepticism. How can we be sure that the clever writer has happened on the right clue to the character he undertakes to reveal to us?

In the "Mirrors of Downing Street," and "Painted Windows," and "Uncensored Celebrities," we have interesting studies of character. We have snap-shots of distinguished statesmen and churchmen. But do we really get inside the minds of these persons; and, if we did, should we be as wise as we think we should be?

Take this question in regard to Mr. Lloyd George. The writer, speaking of that statesman's sudden change of front, asks, "How came it that the most pronounced pacifist of a pacifist Liberal Cabinet, who had, six weeks before, begun a passionate crusade against armaments, on the fateful August 4, 1914, gave his voice for war?"

Now, I venture to say that no biographer, furnished with the latest instruments of psychological precision, exploring the recesses of Mr. Lloyd George's mind, but ignoring the tremendous events of crowded days, could give the right answer to that question.

Why does it happen that a quiet householder in Kansas, who is shingling his kitchen roof, on a summer afternoon is seen the next moment frantically digging himself out of a mass of débris? You cannot understand the sudden change of occupation by an intensive study of the Kansas mind — you have to take into account the nature of a cyclone.

The student of Mr. Lloyd George's mind says: "He is always readier to experience than to think. To him the present tick of the clock has all the dignity of the Eternal. If thought is a malady, he is of all men most healthy. The more he advocates a policy, the less he can be trusted to carry it through."

This is clever analysis, but the question intrudes, How does the writer know so much about what goes on inside of Mr. Lloyd George's mind? Why may he not be doing a good deal of rapid thinking while he is experiencing so vividly? And vhy may not this thought directed to the question of the moment be fairly accurate? Granted that he changed his mind rapidly, did he change it any more rapidly than the circumstances with which he had to deal changed? Granted that he didn't bring anything to its logical conclusion. Amid the tremendous forces that were struggling in the world, could anything be brought to its logical conclusion? There is room here for honest doubt.

The biographer may well sharpen his wits by means of psychology, but he must not allow a formula to stand in the way of an individual. From the rigid supra-lapsarians we are always happy to escape to the biographers, ancient or modern, who are of the humanistic school. In their pages we see characters developing unevenly under the stress of circumstances. We cannot tell what a person is capable of doing till he does it; and even then we are not always sure that we have all his reasons. There is no programme that is followed. Unexpected things are all the time turning up and bringing into play powers which we had not looked for. We are compelled to revise our first impressions both of the man and his times. The more the individual is observed, the more individualistic he appears to be. He becomes less significant as a symbol and more interesting as a personality.

There, for example, is Plutarch's Cato. No attempt is made to analyze his character or to account for his idiosyncrasies. We see him just as he happened to be. He doesn't correspond to any formula. He is just Cato.

Cato was gray-eyed and red-headed. He was a self-made man. He worked hard and liked to wear old clothes when he was in the country. He was fond of turnips and of cabbage. He was very thrifty, and when his slaves began to grow old he sold them to save the depreciation in his property. He disliked flatterers, but was not averse to praising himself. He loved sharp jests. He was a popular orator and a good soldier. When he was elected to office, he put a super-tax on articles of luxury; he cut the pipes by which wealthy householders had surreptitiously drawn water from the public fountains; he reduced the rates of interest on loans, and conducted himself with such outrageous rectitude that all the best people turned against him.

All these incidents have to do with the outward life of Cato. Plutarch is content to set them down with the remark, "Whether such things are proof of greatness or of littleness of mind, let each reader judge for himself." Yet somehow they make the red-headed Roman seem very real to us. We know him in the same way that we know a contemporary. If we were to drop into Rome on election day and be told that the paramount issue was "Anything to beat old Cato," we should feel at home. We should probably vote for Cato, and regret it after the election.

We have this sense of complete reality in the characters of statesmen and soldiers which we come upon in the crowded pages of Clarendon. Here is Clarendon's Hampden. It is the portrait of a gentleman drawn by another gentleman who was his enemy. But one would prefer to have Clarendon as an enemy rather than another man as a friend.

John Hampden "was a gentleman of good family in Buckinghamshire, and born to a fair fortune, and of a most civil and affable deportment. In his entrance into the world he indulged to himself all the license in sports, and exercises, and company, which was used by men of the most jolly conversation. Afterwards he retired to a more reserved and melancholy society, yet preserving his own natural cheerfulness and vivacity, and above all a flowing courtesy to all men. . . . He was of that rare affability and temper in debate, and of that seeming humility and submission of judgment, as if he brought no opinion with him but a desire of information and instruction; but he had so subtle a way of interrogating, and, under the notion of doubts, insinuating his objections, that he left his opinions with those from whom he pretended to learn and receive them. ... He was indeed a very wise man and of great parts and possessed with the most absolute spirit of popularity, that is, the most absolute faculties to govern the people, of any man I ever knew."

In Clarendon's eyes, John Hampden was a very dangerous man. "He begat many opinions and motions, the education of which he committed to other men." Of one thing we are not left in doubt. He was a very great man, though he fought on the wrong side.

"He was very temperate in diet, and a supreme governor over all his passions and affections, and had thereby a great power over other men. He was of an industry and vigilance not to be tired out or wearied by the most laborious; and of parts not to be imposed upon by the most subtle or sharp, and of a personal courage equal to his best parts; so that he was an enemy not to be wished wherever he might have been made a friend." It is after all these qualities have been acknowledged that Clarendon adds: "*His death therefore seemed a great deliverance to the nation.*"

No psychologist by the most painstaking analysis could produce the effect that these words make upon us. We are conscious of John Hampden's personality as a force against which strong men are contending. We not only see the man himself, but we see why some men loved him and others resisted him. He was part of a mighty movement, which he largely directed.

Biography cannot be reduced to a science, but it may rise into the finest of the arts. It is the art of reproducing not merely the incidents of a great man's life, nor the mere elements of his character, but the impression he made on those who knew him best.

LISTENING IN ON THE
IRISH QUESTION

IF the Government of the Irish Free State proves permanently satisfactory to its people, it will deprive the English-speaking world of a subject of conversation that has lasted for more than seven hundred years. It has connected the generations together and made them feel as if they belonged to one acrimonious family circle.

When Adrian IV, the only Englishman who ever sat on the papal throne, issued a bull graciously inviting King Henry II to go over and take possession of Ireland, he set the tongues of people on both sides of the channel to wagging. The controversy has not ceased from that day to this. Many things have happened since Strongbow, the valiant Earl of Pembroke, landed in Ireland in accordance with the papal and royal will. One question after another has been asked, discussed for a while, and been forgotten. But the question of the right of the English to rule Ireland has never been dropped.

In a speech in Dublin in 1866, John Bright

called attention to the fact that, five hundred years before, the Parliament of Kilkenny discussed the question, Why is the King of England not a penny the richer for Ireland? We have been debating that question ever since, said Bright, and we are no further on than they were in those days at Kilkenny.

During all that period, not a single new element was introduced into the controversy, with the exception of the religious animosity that came with the sixteenth century. Neither party changed the subject. The debate was without subtleties. It was a sheer conflict of wills. On the one side was Ireland's will to be a nation; and on the other, England's imperturbable refusal to accept this point of view. Here was a subject that could be discussed for generations, because each party had only to repeat its former assertions.

If a group of intelligent persons from different generations who have lived since the days of Strongbow were gathered in a drawing-room, they would find some embarassment in finding a topic which would be familiar to all. A discussion might be started on the Fifth Crusade, or the commercial policy of the Hanseatic League, or the position of Hampden on ship money, or the claims of the Young Pretender, or the wars of the Spanish Succession. But the amount of information possessed by the company would not be sufficient to make the conversation general.

"What do you think of the question of investitures?" asks an elderly gentleman of the twelfth century.

"What investitures?" replies a gentleman of the nineteenth century — "or did you say investments?"

The conversation drops.

But let somebody ask, "What do you think of the Irish Question?" and everybody begins to talk. In the first place, everybody knows that there is an Irish Question, and after a few minutes' conversation finds that it is the same old question that everybody else knows about. The company is on the easy footing of contemporaries. No matter what generation a person belongs to, he feels perfectly at home. As they all have about the same degree of knowledge, they divide according to temperament. There are those who have made up their minds that the Irish Question can never be settled, and are

rather bored by it, and those who think that it
can be settled, and therefore want to keep things
stirred up. Then there are the moderates who
think that the Irish Question could be settled if
it were not for the Irish.

Ignoring the passage of time, we may listen in
while representatives of different periods express
their opinions. We do not need to exercise our
imaginations, for we have their exact words.

Fortunately, we can go back to the beginning
of the trouble and interview a countryman of
Mr. Lloyd George who was tremendously interested in what was happening in his day, and desirous that posterity should know all about it.

Giraldus Cambrensis was the H. G. Wells of
the twelfth century. He had an alert mind and
a keen scent for the kind of news that had historical value and the kind of history that had a definite news value. He conceived history journal-
istically, and liked to have it brought down to
the minute. When his noble Norman kinsmen,
the Fitzgeralds, followed Strongbow, Earl of
Pembroke, to Ireland, Gerald the Welshman
knew that something was going to happen that
ought to be written up. He held the pen of a
ready writer and resolved to do the writing. He

entered into his task with zeal. The Irish Question appears full-blown.

Giraldus begins his history of the Irish troubles very modestly at the time of the Deluge, though other analysts trace the story back to Cain and his progeny. It seems that Noah had a granddaughter named Cæsara, a very independent young lady who seems to have been the leader of the younger set of the ante-diluvians. Hearing that her grandfather was building an ark which was likely to be unpleasantly crowded with animals, she persuaded about thirty of the members of her set to go over to the Mediterranean, where they built a snug little vessel of their own. They would sail away and find some pleasant island where the troubles of the old world would not follow them. Their motto evidently was, "For ourselves." So they sailed away and at last found the beautiful island of Ireland, where they settled with great content.

But alas! Noah's flood proved universal, and they were all drowned. Giraldus replies to those who doubt this story, "My business is to compile history, not to criticize it."

He gossips amiably about the invasion in which his noble relatives, the Fitzgeralds, figurcd so largely. "O family! O race!" he exclaims, "indeed they are doubly noble drawing their courage from the Trojans and their skill in arms from the French." But he lets it be known that the Fitzgeralds, after conquering the native Irish, are ready to fight any newcomers. He gives the King advice as to how Ireland ought to be governed, and warns him that it is going to be difficult. The Irish people are never so light-hearted as when getting up a rebellion. They have long memories, and they carry a detestable weapon called a broad-axe. They excel in irregular warfare. While the heavily armored Norman knight is getting off his horse, the Irish rebel will be in the bogs, making ready for a new adventure. As for settling the Irish Question, let no one think that it can be done in our day. "The Irish have four prophets whose writings are still extant. They foretold the English invasion. They say the war will last unto the remotest generation. Indeed, they say it will continue till the day of Judgment."

Giraldus concludes his history by saying that he has done his best to bring it up to date; he will leave to others to tell how it all turned out.

It is a far cry from Giraldus Cambrensis in the

twelfth century to John Quincy Adams in the
nineteenth, but if the Irish Question were introduced they would soon be contradicting each
other most vivaciously. Giraldus would find
much to interest him in a volume published in
1834, "Dermot MacMorragh, or the Conquest
of Ireland," by John Quincy Adams. To the ex-
President the conquest of Ireland was a matter
of present concern. Henry II was as real as General Jackson and his conduct was as reprehensi-
ble. Indeed, he seemed to fear that his readers
might not believe in his indignation at the male-
factors of the Middle Ages and think that he was
attacking his American political adversaries.

"Dermot by his subjects was detested
As tyrants like him never fail to be."

He insisted that it was Dermot MacMorragh
who lived in Ireland in the time of Henry II that
he was angry at.

"Give me leave to say that I know best
My own intentions in the lines I trace.
Let no man therefore draw aside the screen
And say 'tis any other that I mean."

Like the old Irish bards Adams ends with a
prophecy:

"Soon, soon shall dawn the day, as dawn it must,
When Erin's sceptre shall be Erin's trust."

John Quincy Adams was not much of a poet,
and we may as well turn to one whose eminence
in that line is undisputed. Let us interview
William Shakespeare:

"Mr. Shakespeare, what do you think of the
Irish Question?"

He would answer, "I'm sure I shouldn't know
what to do without it. It's very convenient in
my business as a playwright. In an historical
play you have to have something in the background that everybody is familiar with. When I
want to get rid of a nobleman of high rank, and
don't want to clutter up the stage with his dead
body, I send him off to the unlucky Irish wars.
This makes a very effective end. It's ever so
much better than having him beheaded or run
through with a sword."

Shakespeare takes the Irish troubles for
granted. They had always been going on,
though nobody cared to ask for the particular
causes of them.

In "Richard II," Willoughby says,

"The King's grown bankrupt, like a broken man."

And Ross answers,

"He hath not money for these Irish wars."

In "Henry IV," Worcester says,

> "What with the absent king,
> What with the injuries of a wanton time,
> And the contrarious winds that held the King
> So long in his unlucky Irish wars!"

Unlucky the Irish wars certainly were in those days for all who engaged in them. Ireland is the land of evil tidings. "The wind sits fair for news to Ireland, but none returns" — at least no good news.

In "Henry VI," the messenger appears with a message familiar to the Plantagenets and the Tudors:

> "From Ireland am I come amain,
> To signify that rebels there are up.
> Send succors, lords, and stop the rage betime,
> Before the wound do grow uncurable."

Of course the Englishmen were ready for reprisals, and a new wound was made.

The victories of Henry V in France could not be celebrated on the stage without the audiences that Shakespeare played for thinking of the Irish war that was then going on and whose issue was still uncertain. The chorus, after describing the glorious victory at Agincourt, expresses the uncertainty of the present.

"Were now the general of our gracious Empress
(As in good time he may) from Ireland coming,
Bringing rebellion broached on his sword,
How many would the peaceful city quit
To welcome him!"

Another Elizabethan poet, Edmund Spenser, had taken part in these Irish wars and had very decided opinions on the Irish Question. He gives them at length in the "Faerie Queene." His patron, Lord Grey of Wilton, was one of the soldiers whose stern measures of repression turned some of the fairest parts of Ireland into a desert. Spenser celebrates him as Sir Artegall, or Justice. Sir Artegall not only uses his sword, but he has with him his serving man Talus, or Force, who with his club beats down the rebellious rabble.

Spenser put his ideas in the form of a dialogue, which might have expressed the opinion of an English gentleman of the early twentieth century as well as of the sixteenth. Two characters are introduced, and we are enabled to listen in as they discuss the question of the day.

"*Eudoxus.* If that country of Ireland from whence you came lately be of so goodly a soil as you report, I wonder that no course is taken to reduce that nation to better government.

"*Ireneaus.* Marry, there have been divers good plots devised, and wise counsels, but they say it is the fatal destiny of that land that no purposes whatsoever that are meant for her good will take effect; whether it is the influence of the stars, or that Almighty God reserves her as a scourge to England, it is hard to know — but much is to be feared.

"*Eudoxus.* That is a vain conceit. I would not impute it to the stars, but to some unsoundness of the counsels laid for the reformation of Ireland, or faintness in following up the same. Still, I have heard some of great wisdom say it were well if that island were dropped into a sea pool. But this seems the kind of speech of desperate men rather than of grave counsellors. If it be not too painful, tell me the troubles of Ireland which hinder the good government thereof.

"*Ireneaus.* Surely, Eudoxus. The evils are as many as were hidden in the basket of Pandora, and many of them are of very great antiquity. And they are daily growing and increasing continually. The evils are of three sorts, — first in the laws, second in the customs, and third in the religion.

"*Eudoxus.* Do they not obey the King's laws in Ireland?

"*Ireneaus.* No, Eudoxus, there are wide countries in Ireland where the King's laws were never established and no acknowledgment of subjection.

"*Eudoxus.* Is there any part that has not been subdued to the crown?

"*Ireneaus.* More than once they have been subdued, but never to perpetual duty. What boots it to break a colt and then let him straight run loose at random? Whenever the Irish are left to themselves, they forget what they have been taught and shake off their bridles.

"*Eudoxus.* But if their ancestors were brought into subjection, should not the present generation acknowledge the same subjection?

"*Ireneaus.* They say not!"

Here you have the conclusion of every argument on the Irish Question. The Englishman presents his statement of facts, and his programme for the future. The answer in each generation is, *They say not.*

The letters of Sir Walter Raleigh teem with bitterness about Ireland. "I hear three thousand Burkes are in arms, and young O'Donnell and Shane O'Neill. I wrote ten days ago of the rebellion, which the Queen made scorn of." To Sir Robert Cecil he writes: "Her Majesty hath good cause to remember that a million has been spent in Ireland not many years ago. A better kingdom could be purchased at less price. This accursed kingdom hath always been a traffic in which Her Majesty hath paid both the freight and the customs. From this devilish place I have little matter and less hope — and the shorter the discourse the better."

To the Earl of Leicester, he says: "I have spent some time here. I will not trouble your honor with the business of this lost land, nor with the good, the bad, the mischiefs, the means to amend, and all in all of this commonwealth or rather this common woe."

From the petulancy of Raleigh, it is a relief to turn to a bright and airy letter of Sir Francis Bacon to James the First in 1606, in which he points the way out. For generations the attempt had been made to bring settlers from England to hold Ireland for the King. In a generation they became Irishmen. The English Pale had been the seat of rebellion. Great families like the Fitzgeralds had forgotten that they were not Irish. But would it not be possible to settle the lands in Ulster, which had been depopulated after the last rebellion, with people who could be counted upon to remain at enmity to the native Irish? What of the Scotch Presbyterians, a stubborn folk, as the King well knew? Difference of religion, which made them troublesome in Great Britain, would make them useful in Ulster.

"What an excellent division is ministered by God's Providence in the state of Ireland! Let there be a discharge of people from England and Scotland into the waste places of Ireland. So shall His Majesty have a double convenience in the avoidance of people here and making use of them there. . . . It is not possible that many of great means will be attracted to Ulster. But their kinsfolks and tenants will have expectation of a great bargain when the wild Irish are driven out."

Bacon becomes sentimental in expounding this great plan: "You shall touch the ancient harp of Ireland and, listening to new tunes and harmonies, the barbarous people will discontinue their customs of revenge and give ear to the wisdom of laws and governments."

This settlement of the Irish Question by the

creation of a New Scotland in Ulster seemed good in the eyes of King James. Ben Jonson celebrates it in the "Irish Masque." He calls upon the people of the troubled island to rejoice.

> "Come up and view
> The gladding face of that great king, in whom
> So many prophecies of thine are knit,
> This is our James of whom long since thou singest
> Shall end our countries' most unnatural broils,
> If but her ear deafened by the drum
> Would stoop but to the music of his peace.
> This is the man thou promised should redeem,
> If she would love his counsels and his laws,
> Her head from servitude, her feet from fall,
> Her fame from barbarism, her state from fall."

This was a large "if." It was soon apparent that the Irish did not love the counsels and the laws of King James. That canny monarch was not unaware of this fact. The plantation of Ulster had involved a good deal of expense, and in order to finance the enterprise a new order, the baronets, was created. Affluent citizens were knighted for a sufficient sum, which they contributed to the royal treasury. At one of these functions, the candidate who was about to be dubbed showed signs of embarrassment. "Don't be abashed, man," said the King; "you have not so much reason to be ashamed of this business as I have."

The relief furnished by the Ulster Plantation was like that experienced by a patient, when by means of local applications his neuralgia is driven from one part of the body to settle permanently in another. While no part of the English-speaking world has been free from occasional twinges in the North of Ireland the irritation has had a constancy that has lifted it into the place of a religion. Good people have become martyrs to their antipathies. There is something liturgical in their objurgations. "Like prayers divine they say each day the very same." It is not a sudden storm that spends itself in fury. It is a steady indignation that floweth like a river. There is an unchangeable conviction that compromise is one of the seven deadly sins.

I pick up a little book published in 1640, entitled "Irish Prognostications," "wherein is described the disposition of the Irish with the manner of their behavior, and how they are for the most part addicted to Popery." Its argument is complete and conclusive.

"A conquest should draw three things after it — law, language, and religion. The vanquished should surrender themselves and imitate the laws, language, and religion of their conquerors. This the Irish will not do."

There you have the Irish Question in a nutshell, or rather in a bombshell. Whenever it is put that way, there is an explosion.

Evidently not much real progress had been made since in the previous century John Derek published "The Image of Ireland," "wherein is most lively expressed the Nature and Qualities of the Wild Irish, their notable aptness, celerity and proneness to rebellion; printed in London for the pleasure and delight of the well disposed."

Derek must have thought that his well-disposed English readers were very easily pleased, for he gives them no reason to believe that their good disposition would be appreciated by the Irish. The Englishman, conscious of his own rectitude, he thinks, does not understand how much the Irish dislike him.

> "The more he seeketh them to win
>   The further off they stray,
>   As imps that do detest to walk
>   The straight and pleasant way."

They even make fun of the serious attempts to improve them.

"They harp upon one string
And therein find a joy,
When as they find a subtle slight
To work true men annoy.
For mockery is their game
Wherein they do delight."

This temperamental difference which was felt in the sixteenth century was only aggravated by the closer contacts brought about in the seventeenth century by the Ulster Plantation.

During the civil wars of the Cromwellian period, as during the Wars of the Roses and the wars of the French Revolution and during the World War of 1914, the Irish patriots were singularly self-absorbed. They were so interested in their own troubles that they were oblivious to what was going on in the rest of the world. It was the story of Noah's granddaughter once again. They were caught in a deluge that swept upon them from overseas. The maxim, "England's extremity is Ireland's opportunity," accounts for a great deal of the Irish ill luck. It has led them, with singular uniformity, to ally themselves in any great crisis with the losing side.

The Irish were against Charles the First and Strafford was sent to repress the disturbance. He was recalled from the unlucky Irish wars, and sent to the scaffold. The Commonwealth was established, and Ireland was unaware of the might of the Puritan till it resisted, and Cromwell's curse fell upon it. The Stuarts were restored, and one would expect better times.

But open Pepys's "Diary," and we hear the same monotonous complaints. "Ireland is in a distracted condition. God knows my heart. I expect nothing but ruin can follow — unless things are better in a little time."

We turn over the leaves of the diary, expecting better news, but affairs grow steadily worse. "Mr. Lewellen, lately come from Ireland, tells how the English interests fall away mightily, the Irish party being too great. Which gives great discontent to the English."

There is another revolution in England. The Stuarts are driven out. When the cause of King James is hopeless, Ireland rises in his behalf, and another unforeseen deluge overwhelms it.

As the South of Ireland has to its own hurt acted on the principle that England's extremity is Ireland's opportunity, so the North has held fast to the principle that Ireland's importunity must be met by Ulster's imperturbability. Ulster stands fast in its integrity. It will not budge. It looks upon compromise as one of the seven deadly sins. Long before the days of Sir Edward Carson, the plucky little province gave its ultimatum. It belonged to the British Empire, and it was willing to fight the whole Empire rather than to allow itself to be put out of it. It would fight for its inalienable right to dependence as sturdily as other nations fought for independence. It was from the very beginning a loyal little eagle, ready to scratch its parents' eyes out if they should ever attempt to shove it out of the nest.

I doubt whether loyalty has ever been more genuine, or has ever taken so troublesome a form. Ulster has stuck to the Empire — like a burr. In the days of the Commonwealth, the burr, like loyalty, almost drove the English Parliament distracted.

In 1649, when Ireland was in a state of chaos, and Ormond was leading a Royalist rebellion, the Presbytery of Belfast passed a series of highly provocative resolutions which it sent to Cromwell. They began in a characteristic manner: "Considering the dependency of this kingdom upon England, we are encouraged to cast our mite into the treasury." The mite consisted of enough explosive materials to blow up all parties. There is first a solemn testimony against all who "labor to establish by law a universal toleration of religion, thus overturning the unity of religion and the first two articles of our solemn covenant." Then there is a denunciation of Parliament which is declared "anti-Christian and Popish, and against the covenant as established by the Church of Scotland, which is now blasphemed."

Under these circumstances, the Presbytery declared its unshakable loyalty to the Government and its determination to express that loyalty in its way, without fear or favor.

"Resolved, that we will not extol the persons of notorious sectaries, the plague of these times, that they may believe lies and be damned.

"We will not be drawn away by counsels, commands, or examples to shake off the ancient government of these kingdoms.

"That we will endeavor the preservation of the Union, remembering the part of the covenant which says, We shall not suffer ourselves directly or indirectly by whatsoever combination or terror to be divided from this blessed union. And finally we exhort every one to avoid all opposers of the reformation, refusers of the covenant, or those who combine with papists. We exhort them not to favor the sectaries, nor incline their hearts to favor the malignants, nor to think they stand in need of the malignants."

As by the "malignants" were meant all who sympathized with the Royalists; and by "notorious sectaries, the plague of these times," the English Independents, who then were in control of the Government, it is not strange that Ulster's mite was not well received.

The resolutions were answered by John Milton in his most vituperative style:

"What mean these men? Is the Presbytery of Belfast, a small town in Ulster, to talk so arrogantly? Are we under the censure of the Presbytery of Belfast?"

He taunts them for their very peculiar kind of loyalty: "These priestlings at the very time their lips disclaimed all sowing of sedition were ready to rebel. News has come that the Scottish inhabitants of Ulster are actually revolted."

The more he thinks about it, the more angry Milton gets:

"These ministers of Belfast, with as much devilish malice, impudence and falsehood as any

Irish, threaten us from their barbarous work in the North of Ireland. . . . These men imagine themselves marvellously high set and exalted in the chair of Belfast to outface the Parliament of Ireland. What are they ministers for, and who set them so haughty in the pontifical see of Belfast, we know not. How dare they send such a defiance? By their actions we might think them a set of highland thieves and red-shanks who, being admitted by the courtesy of England to hold possessions in our province of Ulster, have proved ungrateful and treacherous guests."

We can imagine the grave ministers of Belfast reading this tirade of the English sectary. His accusations of disloyalty were preposterous. Of course, if Parliament disturbed the blessed union and cut them off from dependence on the British Government, Ulster "would fight, and Ulster would be right." From that position, neither they nor their descendants would swerve.

Again we listen in to catch what people of intelligence are saying in regard to the situation in Ireland, in the century after Milton. It is Jonathan Swift, Dean of Saint Patrick's, who is speaking. It appears that the question, Is Ireland a nation? is still a living issue. Swift says:

"They say Ireland is a depending kingdom. I have looked over all the English and Irish statutes without finding any law that makes Ireland depend on England any more than England depends on Ireland. We have been obliged to have the same king with them, and consequently they have been obliged to have the same king with us. . . . In reason all government without the consent of the governed is the very definition of slavery. We have nothing to do with the English ministers, and I would be as sorry if it lay in their power to redress our grievances as to enforce them." He tells the Irishman that, "By the laws of God, of Nature, of nations and of your own country you are and ought to be as free as your brethren in England."

All this seems very modern. If we didn't look at the date, we might think that Dean Swift had read our Declaration of Independence.

A little later we listen in to hear what Dr. Johnson might have to say. The Doctor is never in a good humor when any one tries to draw him out on the Irish Question.

Boswell inquires cautiously, "Would you not like to visit Ireland?"

Johnson: "It is the last place where I should wish to travel."

Boswell: "Should you not like to go to Dublin?"

Johnson: "No, sir."

Boswell: "Is not the Giant's Causeway worth seeing?"

Johnson: "Worth seeing? Yes! But not worth going to see."

But Boswell was not a man who feared being snubbed, and when the moment seemed propitious he continued his inquiries:

"But, Doctor Johnson, do you not believe that a closer union with England would be good for Ireland?"

Johnson: "Sir, it would only give us a better chance to rob them."

Boswell: "But union with Scotland has worked well. You haven't robbed us."

Johnson: "Sir, the only reason we haven't robbed Scotland is because there isn't anything worth taking."

This was during the time of Grattan's Parliament, when Ireland was for a time granted Home Rule with a string to it. The Irish Parliament had the right to talk in Dublin, while the legislating was done at Westminster.

At no period was the Irish Question more

exasperating to people who were striving for a
reasonable solution. In 1780, Edmund Burke
writes: "I have had my holiday of popularity in
Ireland. I have heard of an intention to erect a
statue to me. I am glad it never took effect. The
fragments of the piece might see service while
they are moving according to the law of projec-
tiles against the windows of my friends."

As for the attempts of the Government to
adopt a policy of conciliation after coercion
had failed, he says, "The awkward parade of
tricking out necessity in the garments of choice,
the shallow stratagem of defending by argument
what is yielded to force, these are things not to
my mind."

Coming down to the early years of the nineteenth century, we find Walter Scott meditating
on the old question. Writing to Joanna Baillie,
he tells her of the impressions made upon a
friendly visitor:

"I had intended to write about Ireland. But
alas, Hell is paved with good intentions. I never
saw a richer country, or to speak my mind a
finer people — but how they do dislike one another! Their factions have been so long enven-
omed and they have such a narrow ground to

battle in. They are like people fighting with dag-
gers in a hogshead. The Protestants of the North
are a fine race — but dangerous to the quiet of
the country."

As for the particular issue of the day over
which they were violently contending, Scott
says:

"I do not believe either party cares much
about it. The Catholics desire it because the
Protestants are not willing they should have it.
The Protestants desire to withhold it because
they think it mortifies the Catholics."

Can it be that this long-drawn-out controversy, which was two hundred years old when
the Turks took Constantinople, and which has
gone querulously and angrily ever since, has
come to an end? Can it be that the Irish Question is in danger of becoming a matter of purely
historical interest? Must there in the future be
learned footnotes to explain the allusions to it in
English literature? Has it come to such a pass
that it ceases to be a stand-by for those who try
to start conversations?

Two years ago, this seemed impossible. Now
it seems likely. The treaty with the Irish Free

State introduced a new idea. There was an abrupt change of subject.

The old question had been, What right had England, or, if you will, the British Empire, to govern Ireland? This question was dropped by the tacit consent of both parties. Instead, another question was propounded: Would it not be for the advantage of Ireland to belong to the British Commonwealth of Nations?

It is this conception of a commonwealth of equal nations, united for mutual protection and bound together by common interests and affections, that has taken the place of the British Empire which Kipling celebrated. Of course, Ireland is a nation, and so is England, and so is Scotland, and so is Canada. These nations, each cherishing its own history and developing its own institutions, are members of one great Commonwealth.

The idea of such a new relation kindled the imagination of Michael Collins and made him willing to try an experiment that had not been tried before. Thousands of his countrymen have caught the same vision. When they come to discuss the proper relations of the Irish nation to the commonwealth of nations to which it belongs, new questions will arise. They will prove to be more interesting than the recapitulation of old feuds. A new generation is likely to arise which will ask, What *was* the Irish Question?

THE LITERARY TASTES OF MY GREAT-GRANDMOTHER

In my old family Bible is the record of the birth of my grandmother: Amanda Dunlap, born May 26, 1802. She was born in a pioneer's cabin on the banks of the Ohio River.

The birth record tells all I know of the literary tastes of my great-grandmother. She had been bred in the Virginia mountains and had come down into the great valley of the Ohio. She was familiar with the perils of the wilderness, and was not afraid of wildcats and Indians. Books were not plentiful in the backwoods of America, yet she had shed tears over the book which fashionable ladies in London were weeping over at the same time. I like to think that her emotions were up to date.

It was in 1798 that "The Children of the Abbey" was published. Four years later, my great-grandmother named her first-born daughter Amanda. She was one of a regiment of Amandas named after the best seller of the day. I take up "The Children of the Abbey" and am at once introduced to the adorable and tender-hearted

Amanda. She is coming up the driveway in a chaise. When she reaches her nurse's cottage, she begins an apostrophe:

" 'Hail, sweet asylum of my infancy. Hail, ye venerable trees. My happiest hours of childish gayety were passed beneath your shelter. Here unmolested may I wait till the rude storm of sorrow is overblown.' Such were the words of Amanda, as she turned down a little verdant lane to her nurse's cottage. A number of tender recollections rushing upon her mind rendered her almost unable to alight."

That was just like Amanda — she kept acting in that way all through the book. She was a creature of palpitating sensibility, with feelings so delicate that they responded to every breath. Amanda was beautiful to a fault, and most beautiful when in tears. When in doubt she always fainted, and there was always some one to sustain her in these emergencies.

Amanda never knew her own mind: that would have been unmaidenly. She was all pure feeling which never fell into anything so vulgar as common sense. She knew that she was lovely, but that did not make her proud; it only made her exquisitely timid.

Her habitual attitude is that of adorable embarrassment. It doesn't matter what it is, it has the same effect on Amanda. When she is introduced to Lord Mortimer, "Her conscious eyes were instantly bent on the ground, a crimson glow was suddenly succeeded by a deadly paleness, and her head sunk on her bosom."

Of course, she fell madly in love with Lord Mortimer, who fell madly in love with her. But when the course of true love threatened to run smooth, the lovers invented all sorts of impediments to make rough water. Whenever there was a chance of misunderstanding, they misunderstood. Whenever a word would have straightened everything out, "Delicacy sealed the lips of Amanda and she blushed violently." This, of course, always upset Lord Mortimer, and rendered his judgment unreliable.

Whenever, for the moment, things seemed to be going well with Amanda, she had a presentiment that it was preparatory to a change for the worse. After Lord Mortimer had assured her in the plainest terms of his undying affection, "Amanda returned to her chamber in a greater state of happiness than she had ever experienced — and immediately burst into tears. For it was a happiness that agitated rather than soothed her. Her feelings were acutely susceptible to every impression.

"They turned at the touch of joy and woe,
And turning trembled too."

As for Lord Mortimer, the spotless hero, his sensibilities were as acute as Amanda's, if not more so. When anything was to be done, you could count on Lord Mortimer for not doing it. His feelings always interfered and tripped him up. At a crucial moment, we are told, "Lord Mortimer trembled universally and was compelled to have recourse to his handkerchief to hide his emotion." When his lordship emerged from his handkerchief, the time for action had passed.

So the story goes on for several hundred pages. There are blushes and fainting spells and tearful reconciliations. There is only one character who knows his own mind, and that is the wicked Colonel Belgrave, who is bent on abducting Amanda. He pursues his object with a pertinacity and ingenuity that does credit to his understanding, though not to his moral nature.

At last fortune favors the innocent, and all their enemies come to a bad end. The hero and the heroine are vindicated and there seems to be nothing to interfere with the wedding. One would suppose that Lord Mortimer would cheer up, but habit is too strong for him — and he once more bursts into tears.

"'These tears, these emotions, O Mortimer, what do they declare?' exclaimed Amanda. It was long before Lord Mortimer could compose his agitation in order to explain. Alternately he fell at the feet of Amanda, alternately he folded her to his bosom and asked his heart if the present happiness was real."

It was then that for the first time in the book Amanda did the sensible thing. "Amanda now made a strong effort to calm her own agitation in order to soothe Lord Mortimer into tranquillity; and at length she succeeded."

It is evident that if Amanda had made that strong effort at any time before, she could have straightened out her affairs. But then I remember that if the heroine of "The Children of the Abbey" had been endowed with ordinary common sense instead of being a creature of extraordinary sensibility, the book would never have reached the banks of the Ohio River, and my grandmother's name would not have been Amanda.

While English duchesses and American pioneers were weeping over the self-inflicted woes of Lord Mortimer and Amanda, the French reading public was in a like tearful mood. The term "French novel" had no suggestion of realism or of cynical cleverness. All was innocence and tender feeling. Who could resist the tale of Paul and Virginia on the West Indian island? They were at once children of Nature and paragons of refinement. They burst into tears on the slightest provocation, and so did Madame La Tour, who was old enough to have known better.

In the last half of the eighteenth century, sentimentalism flowed like a river. Miss Anna Seward, the swan of Litchfield, laved in it. The one test of a popular book was that it left the reader bathed in tears.

I pick up a volume published in 1772, entitled "Sentimental Fables, designed for the use of ladies." In the preface the author declares his intention to be sentimental to the point of ruthlessness. "The author has attempted to affect the heart and excite the passions, to adorn sentiment with elegance and harmonious versification, and express virtue in such an easy and flowing style as to make it agreeable to those of

refined taste, especially to those of the gentler
sex."

Falling naturally into poetry, he exclaims:

"The heart that now these strains indites,
With friendly warmth the hand that writes,
Must cease to move and soon become
The food of reptiles in the tomb.
Yet when against my dauntless breast
The viper foe shall rear his crest,
Then to have strove will cheer my heart
To adorn creation's nobler part
By pleasing tales to let them know
Virtue's the only good below."

It is the same feeling that animates the "Ode
to Sensibility," which begins:

"The youth that carols to the moon his lays
As inoffensive as the song he loves."

In the Golden Age of Sentimentalism, inoffen-
siveness was a cardinal virtue.

Here is a poem published in Edinburgh in
1772 and dedicated to Rousseau. It is entitled
"The Sentimental Sailor." The preface says:

"The author of the following poem is impelled
by the irresistible impulse of awakened sensibility. The story of the nightingale singing with
her breast against a thorn may with sufficient
propriety be applied to my muse. Poetry is

never so flowing and so universally pleasing and harmonious as when, inspired by deep distress, she utters in the language of Nature the voice of unavailing woe."

There you have the doctrine of the sentimental school. To have literary value, the woe must not only be deep; it must be unavailing.

The sentimental sailor feels that it is his duty to keep himself as unconsolable as possible. He doesn't explain what his trouble is. It is not even clear that he was disappointed in love, but it was evident that he loved to be disappointed. He is very ingenious in escaping any alleviations to his miserable lot. Whenever the skies begin to clear, he sails away indignantly in search of a tornado. As long as he is on blue water, he can be sure of a disturbance. Even on land he can make his sorrows vocal.

> "On Libyan wilds a lion fierce, I'd roar,
> Or while around the famished monsters howl
> On fields of ice a surly bear I'd growl.
> With sudden joy I greet the stormy cloud.
> Ye tempest blow, ye mountain billows roll.
> Welcome the gloom congenial to my soul.
>
> To soothe my raging griefs with fancied woes
> Pensive, alone with tardy pace I go
> To where no human footsteps mark the ground
> To vast sequestered solitude profound."

I turn to the works of the poet Mallet, now long forgotten, I find "Verses written for and given in print to a beggar." The verses begin, "O mercy, heaven's first attribute!"

There you have the very quintessence of sentimentalism. I can fancy the poet thinking over the problem of poverty and what he could do to abate it. At last a happy thought strikes him. He will write a poem on Mercy and have it printed, and he will bestow it on the beggars whom he meets on the London streets. I like to think of the poet distributing his literary benefactions.

Here is another once popular poet, whose name is not now familiar, Hammond. He has a large number of poems in honor of Delia. One series is explained. "He imagines himself married to Delia and that, content with each other, they retire into the country." This makes a very good beginning. He is full of good resolutions.

> "With timely care I'll sow my little field,
>   And plant my orchard with its master's hand,
>   Nor blush to spread the hay, the hook to wield,
>   And range the sheaves along the sunny land."

This seems very promising in Delia's husband;

but his account of what he intends to do in the hot growing weather awakens our fears. He evidently does not intend to spoil his complexion by ordinary work in the fields. He will,

> "If the sun in flaming Leo ride,
> By shady rivers indolently stray,
> And with my Delia walking by my side
> Hear how they murmur as they glide away.
> With joy to wind along the cool retreat
> And stop to gaze at Delia as I go."

But there must be some drudgery even on a poet's farm. The question arises who is to do it? In a few lines further, the sentimental poet reveals the fact that he will let Delia do it.

> "Hers be the care of all my little train
> While I with tender indolence am blest."

In the Golden Age of Sentimentalism an atmosphere of tender indolence seems to surround the youth of both sexes. The young ladies of the period were in continual need of support.

"What has influenced you, my dear Miss Milner?" was asked of a young lady in Mrs. Inchbald's "Simple Story."

" 'That which impels all my instincts — a fatality which renders me the most miserable of human beings.'

"At this sentence she sat down on a chair that was close to her. Her feet could not have taken her to any other. She trembled, she was white as ashes and deprived of speech."

Was Miss Milner as unhappy as her physical symptoms would indicate? We do not know. All that we can be sure of is that, like all the young ladies of fiction in her period, she had cultivated the will to faint.

Fanny Burney, the author of "Evelina," when she was maid of honor to Queen Charlotte, was able to stand for hours in the presence of royalty, and walk backward without tripping. But in her "Wanderer," or "Female Difficulties," we find no character who is capable of such feats. They all find difficulty in retaining their equilibrium under the stress of emotion.

"'O, appease the raging ferment in my veins,' cried Elinor.

"She opened the window and leaned out her head. Harleigh, in a universal tremor, clapping his hands and his crimsoned forehead, walked with hasty steps around the room. Elinor lost all self-command, wringing her hands in ungovernable anguish.

"'My dear Elinor, compose yourself,' cried

Harleigh." Harleigh ought to have known better than to make that suggestion. It was the last
thing Elinor intended to do.

"A paleness like that of death overspread her
face. Her voice faltered, she shook so violently
that she could not support herself. She put her
hand gently on the arm of Harleigh, and gliding
nearly behind him leaned upon his shoulder.
Then, recovering herself, she was covered with
blushes, and addressing Harleigh she said, 'Par-
don, Mr. Harleigh, this terrible crisis must be
my apology.'

"Tears rolled down Elinor's cheeks as she
ejaculated, 'I hail thee again, O Life! Welcome,
welcome every evil that associates my catastrophe with that of Harleigh. Yet I blush, me-
thinks, to live. I feel so little.'"

"With these words, and receding from a solemn yet tender exhortation begun by Harleigh,
she abruptly quitted the building, and her mind,
not more highly wrought by self-exaltation than
her body, weakened by successive emotions, she
was compelled to accept the fearfully offered
assistance of Ellis to regain, with tottering steps,
the house."

One sympathizes with the sternly prosaic

Madame Schwellenberg, Queen Charlotte's mistress of the robes, when Fanny Burney, with her reputation as a popular novelist still fresh, was introduced into the Queen's inner circle. When a gentleman was introduced to read aloud to the ladies —

"Mrs. Schwellenberg desired him to read and had a standing desk procured such as is used by readers to the Queen, who are not, of course, allowed to sit down.

"'What book is it to be, ma'am, something interesting, I hope?'

"' No,' cried she, 'I won't have nothing what you call novels, what you call romances, what you call histories. I might not read what you call stuff.'

"The good Mrs. Planta, a Swiss by birth and good-humored, feared that I might look upon this speech as a personal reflection, and to soften it said, 'O Miss Burney, what pretty books you write. I cry at it. I cry just like a little baby.' But Mrs. Schwellenberg was firm, and the book which was read that day was 'Josephus.'"

There is a great deal to be said in behalf of Mrs. Schwellenberg's choice of books. It was her duty to keep the young ladies and gentlemen of

the Court of George III in training for the very
arduous duties involved in the etiquette of their
position. If they must read something, Mrs.
Schwellenberg felt that "Josephus" was better
for their nerves than what she called stuff.

Were people more sentimental in the days
when "The Children of the Abbey" was read
with tears than they are now? Yes! — in their
novel-reading hours. For the rest of the time
they seem to have had their nerves under remarkably good control. It was the age of Dr.
Johnson and George Washington and Benjamin
Franklin. I doubt very much whether my great
grandmother ever found a time when fainting
from excess of emotion would have seemed the
proper thing.

The study of novels or poems is not an infalli-
ble way to learn the manners or events of a period. So much depends on the fashions in literature. A person with the pen of a ready writer can
vividly describe things which he has never seen.
Thomas Campbell writes,

"On Erie's banks where tigers steal along."

This does not prove that any traveler ever told

Campbell that there were tigers on the shores of Lake Erie. It only proves that in those days a poet put any animals into his landscape which he thought would add interest to it. In his "Gertrude of Wyoming" he pictured the Pennsylvania frontier settlement as having all the romantic accessories of the Old World.

> "Delightful Wyoming, beneath thy skies
> The happy shepherd swains had naught to do
> But feed their flocks in green declivities,
> Or skim perchance thy lake with light canoes,
> From morn till evening's sweeter pastimes grew.
> Thy lovely maidens would the dance renew,
> And aye the sunny mountains halfway down
> Would echo flageolets from some romantic town.
> Not far away some Andalusian saraband
> Would sound to many a native rondelay."

When "Gertrude of Wyoming" reached Pennsylvania, the fair reader would say, "How beautiful!" But this did not prove that she had ever heard an Andalusian saraband in her native State.

The fashions in literature are like fashions in dress. They come and go according to their own laws. We cannot say that the new fashion is better or worse than the old; it is sufficient to note the fact that it is different.

In a book of fugitive poems published in 1745 a young lady of fashion tosses her head as she thinks of the past.

> "Our grandmothers, they tell us, wore
> Their farthingales and their bandore,
> Their pinions forehead cloth and ruff,
> Content with their own cloth and stuff.
> I hate old things and age, I see
> These times are good enough for me,
> The goldsmiths now are very neat,
> I love the air of Lombard Street.
> Whate'er a ship from India brings,
> Pearls, diamonds, silks, are pretty things,
> The cabinet, the screen, the fan
> Please me extremely from Japan.
> And what affects me still the more
> They had none of these things heretofore."

This is an illusion dear to the heart of the youth of each generation — "they had none of these things heretofore." This is the force which drives every fashion to an extreme.

At the present time the fashion in novels is strongly, even savagely unsentimental. Many of our most admired authors manifest a cold animosity toward their characters. They, poor creatures, have done nothing to deserve it. The author of their being turns against them. He will not shed tears over their failures, or rejoice over their small successes. He does not even allow them to be amusing. His business is to show them up. As for the communities in which they live, their smugness and narrowness are portrayed by a hand that never relents. The author will let no guilty town escape.

But what does this prove about the actual life of America? What if in these small towns there should be big-hearted, keen-witted citizens, with a zest for life and a great capacity for rational enjoyment? And what if, in many cases, their fellow citizens, instead of freezing them out should be proud of them?

In that case, says the fashionable novelist of the severer school, you have material for the biographer or the historian. Such characters do not appeal to the writer of serious fiction in these days. If you want another kind of novel you must wait till the fashion changes or else go back to your old favorites.

NEW POETS AND POETS
NOT SO NEW

BEN JONSON, in giving his comedy of the "New Inn" to the press, appeals to the quiet reader against the judgment of the fashionable theatergoers who had damned his play on the first night. From the security of the printed page he defies his enemies.

"What did they come for? I will partly answer. They came to see and be seen, to make a general muster of themselves in clothes bought on credit, and to possess the stage against the play by rising between the acts in oblique lines to make affidavit to the world that they did not understand one scene." The poet was like a lawyer demanding a change of venue.

"Reader, if such thou be, I make thee my patron and dedicate the piece to thee, for thy better literature. I trust myself and my book to thy rustic candor rather than to the pomp and pride of their solemn ignorance. Fare thee well! Fall to! Read!"

That was some three hundred years ago. One generation of theater-goers after another has passed away, each with its own standard of taste. But the printed page remains. We take up the book and are contemporaries of Ben Jonson, and hear his great voice booming at us. "Reader! Fall to! Read!"

And because we are readers and not an audience gathered in a theater to greet a particular actor, we obey. A book is new which we have never read before. The passing of a thousand years between the writing and the reading is an irrelevancy.

This is a matter which the new poets and their friends are in danger of forgetting. Here is one who writes of the sudden change that has taken place in poetic values:

"We have revolted against the horrible boredom of exploded tradition. The old conventionalities are of no use to us. They give no sustenance and we turn from the old ways of apprehending beauty and are in open rebellion against all accepted standards. We refuse to do the old stunts. Life is now open to us on all sides. I am elated with the experience, which shows how completely we have stood existence on its head."

Now, this is a very natural feeling, and there

is an exhilaration in the fact that one has stood existence on its head. But there is one thing which the poet should remember, and that is that, whether he is scornfully rejecting the old stunts or confidently practicing the new, he never has the stage to himself. He must compete with the poets of all generations on equal terms. It is all very well to talk about being "in open rebellion against all accepted standards," but as a matter of fact there are no accepted standards in literature. There is only a free field for all comers. The newcomer cannot escape the comparison with those who had arrived before him. Chronology has really very little to do with the matter. An actor competes only with men of his own generation. A poet has no such protection for the product of his brain.

If I were a poet, I should request my friends and admirers to omit the adjective "new" when speaking of me. It is indeed a great privilege to be alive and to have opportunity for future activities. But the accident of my nativity has, I should tell them, nothing to do with poetical values. Nor should my conformity or non-conformity to the literary fashion of the hour be taken into account. If I were a pugilist or a baseball player, I should be compared with my coevals; but as the practitioner of a timeless art, I cannot recognize an age limit. There is no champion so old that he may not "come back."

Such an understanding would give the contemporary poet an equality before the law which is greatly to be desired. He would no longer be praised or blamed for mere vagaries of taste. The old-fashioned reader need no longer condemn him because he does not conform to the standards of his immediate predecessors.

The old-fashioned reader often feels that poetry is in a bad way. For one thing, the distinction between prose and verse is being broken down. He used to know what poetry looked like by glancing at the page, but now he cannot be quite sure. He feels as he does when some one puts salt in the sugar bowl and sugar in the salt cellar. Each is good in its way, but he cannot tell which is which.

Here is an excellent poet, Robert Frost, writing about a woodpile:

> "It was a cord of maple cut and split
> And piled — four by four, by eight."

The dimensions are correctly given, and it would be proper to mention them if he were selling the wood, but the old-fashioned reader asks, Is it necessary to be so exact in poetry? Was it not Shelley who said that "nothing that can be equally well expressed in prose that is not tedious and supererogatory in verse"? And Shelley ought to know.

He is asked to admire Mr. Fletcher's lines on "The Well." He is told that the waters are tainted and that a man went down to clean it once.

> "He found it very cold and deep
> With a queer niche in one of its sides
> From which he hauled forth buckets of brick and dirt."

This is all very well, he says, as an introduction. It tells what the poem's about. Now let's have the poem. The answer is, This is the poem. It's wonderfully suggestive.

"Yes, but what does it suggest?"

"The well. Can't you see it?"

The old-fashioned reader grumbles over the change that has come over the poets. "How different from the poems of my youth!"

> "The old oaken bucket, the iron-bound bucket,
> The moss-covered bucket that hung in the well."

Anybody could tell that was poetry. It looked like poetry when you read it in the school reader, and it sounded like poetry when, with a lilt, you recited it on the school platform. And the poet was not above his business. He told us just what it was intended to suggest, namely, "How dear to my heart are the scenes of my childhood" — and it did.

Poetry should sound differently from prose.

"Curfew shall not ring to-night."

That's poetry.

"The usual ringing of the bell at nine P.M. will be omitted this evening."

That's a church notice.

The complaint is made that present-day poets delight in choosing subjects which shock preconceived ideas as to what is the proper material for poetry. There is Vachel Lindsay writing about "The golden whales of California, Kalamazoo, the Daniel Jazz, and John L. Sullivan the Strong Boy of Boston." There is no objection to celebrating a man from Boston in verse, but could he not have chosen another Bostonian?

I think most of us sympathize with the old-fashioned reader when we take up Carl Sandburg's "Chicago Poems." While we admit his power, we feel a certain lack of urbanity in his greeting.

> "Hog butcher of the world,
> Tool maker, stacker of wheat,
> Player with railroads, nation's freight handler,
> Stormy, husky, brawling,
> City of the big shoulders."

Sandburg evidently believes in treating his readers rough. He slaps us on the back, rolls us in the mud, shows us sights we don't want to see, introduces us to people we don't want to know, and then asks us how we like Chicago.

To sit "with a dynamiter at supper in a German saloon eating steak and onions" is a broadening experience. But the description of it seems to lend itself to prose rather than to poetry. We read:

> "I knew an ice handler who wears a flannel shirt with pearl
> buttons the size of a dollar,
> And he lugs a hundred pound hunk into a saloon box and
> helps himself to cold ham and rye bread."

Is that the way to begin a poem?

We see men digging for the gas mains and watch them as they pause to pull their boots out of "the suck holes where they slosh." We remember Gray's lines on the "Progress of Poesy":

"Now the rich stream of music winds along,
Deep, majestic, smooth and strong."

Then we repeat, "The suck holes where they slosh." Is that sloshing sound poetry?

Speaking of Gray reminds us of the "Elegy Written in a Country Churchyard," which we had committed to memory in our youth. We murmur,

"Beneath these rugged elms that yew trees shade,"

and go on with the melodious lines about the village Hampdens and the mute, inglorious Miltons. Then we turn to Mr. Masters's meditations on a cemetery in the Mississippi Valley. Alas, in Spoon River there were no Hampdens and no Miltons, mute or otherwise. The poet would have us believe that the Spoon Riverites were just ordinary people. If so, we understand the vulgar contraction of the word into "ornery." Of the two hundred and fourteen deceased citizens, few rise above the level of the unlamented Cooney Potter, who died at the early age of sixty-one "from smoking red eagle cigars and gulping coffee."

The old-fashioned reader asks, "In order to keep up with the times, is it necessary to con-

sider the 'Spoon River Anthology' an advance
on the 'Elegy Written in a Country Churchyard'?"

No, dear reader. It is not necessary even to
compare them. The first point of literary justice
is to compare a writer with those of his own class
and whose aims are similar. We do injustice to
compare one who aims to tell the bitter truth in
regard to an unpleasant subject with one who
aims to please. The "Spoon River Anthology"
isn't pleasant reading, and the author didn't
intend it to be such. The question is, Does it
produce the effect he intended? Is it good of its
kind?

Of course there remains the other question,
Do we like the kind? That is a question for the
reader. If he doesn't like the kind, he may decline to read the book, and in so doing is well
within his rights.

Why not compare the "Spoon River Anthology" with grimly realistic poetry of its own
kind? I take up the "Mirror for Magistrates,"
written by a syndicate of writers in the days of
"Bloody Mary." The poets hit upon the same
idea that occurred to Mr. Masters, but instead
of a Middle-West community, they introduce us

to a score or more of characters taken from the history books. Each worthy is made to confess his sordid misdemeanors and misfortunes.

"How King Humber was drowned 1086 B.C."
"How Elstrode, the concubine of King Locrenius, was drowned by Queen Gwendolin, 1064 B.C."
"How King Chiron died of drunkenness, 196 B.C."

We are spared no unpleasant detail. King Chiron tells us all his symptoms:

> "Although my face is fallen, prest and pale
> And legs with dropsy swell,
> Yet let me tell what vice did me confound."

And he does.

King Bland, who broke his neck in the year 844 B.C., is equally insistent that posterity should not have too high an opinion of him. He beseeches the sixteenth-century poet not to cover up any of his transgressions:

> "I pray thee, Higgins, take in hand thy pen
> And write my life, and fall away the rest
> A warning set me down for curious men."

Here we are on the broad highway of realistic poetry. It is poetry with a preference for the seamy side of things. We are able to compare poets who happen to live in different centuries but who practice the same art.

We soon come down to the end of the eighteenth century and meet with Crabbe, who is still the master of this school. Crabbe undertakes to show us, not what is beautiful, but what is severely true. He gives us a picture of the English villages and boroughs as he saw them.

> "Fled are the times when in harmonious strains
> The rustic poet praised his native plains.
> . . . . I paint the cot
> As Truth would paint it and the bards will not."

He paints not only the cottage, but the almshouse, the jails, the overcrowded tenements, and the miserable streets. He makes us acquainted with the citizens of every degree, and he is seldom complimentary. He refuses to accept the conventional rule to say nothing but good of the dead. Looking on the eulogistic inscription on the tombstone of a wealthy citizen, he meditates.

> "On this stone appears
> How worthy he, how virtuous, how dear,
> See, he was liberal, kind, religious, wise.
> . . . . All this of Jacob Holmes.
> What is the truth, old Jacob married thrice
> He dealt in coals, and avarice was his vice.

He ruled the borough when his year came on,
And some forgot, and some are glad he's gone.
For never yet with shilling could he part,
For when it left his hand it struck his heart."

After Crabbe came Ebenezer Elliott, the poet
of the poor. In "The Splendid Village," we see
misery in its stark reality. The man who in his
long absence has idealized his native English
village, returns to find his kinsman reduced to
a poverty that has destroyed all natural feeling.

"He took my offered hand, but froze me with a look.
I came to meet a man, but found a stone.
His wife in tatters watched a fireless grate,
The boys sat near him all in fierce debate
And all in rags."

The unrelieved bleakness of the scene reminds
one of Sandburg's "Mag." The aim of the two
poets was the same — not to please us, but to
awaken us to the existence of facts which we like
to hide from ourselves.

As for the search for unusual subjects which
shock the fastidious, the new poets of our day
are not worse offenders than their predecessors.
Robert Burns has a poem on "The Toothache."
The poem is not very pleasant, neither is the
toothache. No twentieth-century realist could

be more regardless of good taste in the choice of a subject than Burns when he wrote his excellent lines, "To a louse on seeing one on a lady's bonnet in church."

The eighteenth century has a reputation for literary conventionality, but clever writers were always thinking up ways of being unconventional. Cowper writes lines "on the high price of fish." He writes on a barrel of oysters which had been delayed in shipment, in a strain that would please the most modernistic.

> "The barrel was magnificently large,
> But being sent to Olney at free charge
> Was not inserted in the driver's list,
> And therefore overlooked, forgot or missed."

The six books of "The Task" were written to prove that any subject could be a proper theme of poetry.

> "I sing the Sofa, I who lately sang
> Truth, Hope and Charity, and touched with awe
> The solemn chords and with a trembling hand
> Escaped with pain from the adventurous flight,
> Now seek repose upon a humbler theme."

It was not so hard to write a long poem about a sofa, for it suggested to the poet that it might be a pleasant thing to leave this place of rest and take an invigorating walk in the country. In following this suggestion, his muse was much refreshed.

A generation earlier, Alexander Pope chose as his subject a wisp of hair. The "Rape of the Lock" begins,

"Slight is the subject, but not so the praise."

This might be taken as a text for all new poets in search of originality.

Pope's contemporary, Phillips, gained applause for a poem entitled "Cider." The older poets had written in praise of wine, but hadn't thought of cider. In choosing the homely beverage, Phillips felt that he was fluttering the dovecotes of conventional inebriety.

At the same time, Dr. Samuel Garth published a long poem on the "Dispensary," with a highly allegorical account of various drugs. Poets had written on palaces and cottages, but the dispensary had never been used as the subject of poetry.

A generation before that, when Harvey's discovery of the circulation of the blood was the greatest scientific sensation, an admirable poet, Phineas Fletcher, had written the "Purple Is-

land," which was simply an account of the circulation of the blood, rendered in the Spenserian
style.

The complaint against our contemporary
poets, that they search for unusual subjects
which shock the taste of the fastidious, can be
summarily dismissed. In this respect they are
neither better nor worse than their predecessors.
Of course the best poets in their happiest moments do not rack their brains to find subjects
which have not been treated before. The old
themes become alive and beautiful when touched
by them. This is real originality. But even good
poets have their off days, and then they become
restless and seek to make up for waning inspiration by writing on something which nobody
had thought of before. They are like the farmers
who had so much to do with the settlement of
the West. After one or two bumper crops, they
would feel that the soil was being exhausted. Instead of adopting better methods of cultivation,
they would sell out and wander forth in search
of new land that had never been under the
plough. These itinerant agriculturists did not
always improve their condition; but they were
happier than if they had cultivated their old

farms with diminishing returns for their labor.

A critic of the sixteenth century writes: "Among the innumerable sortes of Englyshe Books, and infinite fardels and printed pamphlets wherewithe this countrey is pestered, all shoppes stuffed and every study furnished the greatest parte I thinke in any one kinde are such as are either meere Poeticall, or which tende in some respect (as either in matter or forme) to Poetry."

In such periods of overproduction there is the temptation for the poet to seek some novel way of attracting attention; but this has nothing to do with the real value of his work. Keats put the case admirably when he said that the subject which a poet chooses is like the twig to which the spider attaches her web. Any twig will do, for the web is drawn, not out of the twig, but out of the substance of the spider. Any subject may be choosen — provided only that one is a poet.

If this suggestion were followed, it would do away with many recriminations between poets old and new. The poet, *as poet*, can do no wrong. It is his prosaic double who lodges in the same brain who must be held responsible for any lapses. The theories of this prosaic collaborator are taken by the discerning reader for what they are worth. They do not interfere with the enjoyment of the poetry.

Many innovations which are admired or resented are remarkably superficial. Thus we do not produce an American school of poetry by so simple a device as giving the names of new American towns to poems whose themes may be as old as the hills. The desire of the poet to put his home town on the literary map is a laudable one. It is a form of local patriotism that is seen in familiar hymn tunes like "Brattle Street" and "Federal Street" and "Bangor."

In America the center of the population of poets has moved westward, from New England to Indiana and from Indiana to the geographical center of the country. Nebraska set the example of States' rights in appointing a poet laureate of its own, and its example has been followed. But if the poets of the West insist too stridently on the glories of their own localities there is nothing really new in this. They are in the line of an old tradition.

Turn to Michael Drayton's "Polyolbion," and you will see what mighty efforts were made in the sixteenth century to induce the poetically minded Englishman to "see England first." Drayton was disgusted at the way British poets sought their inspiration in foreign countries.

"Reader, I know thou wouldst rather (because it asks thy labor) remain where thou art rather than walk over England. But let me tell you, reader, the fault lies in your idleness, rather than my want of industry."

How familiar that sounds! The more impatient advocates of new poetry in every age have adopted that chiding tone in addressing the public, which is always inclined to take its literature too lazily.

Drayton was one of the most industrious of all poets. His plan was to make a topographical survey of England and Wales for the benefit of worthy poets who were unacquainted with the resources of their own country. He starts with his muse on a pedestrian tour, and whenever he comes to a town or river which has poetical possibilities he makes a note of it. There are thirty books in the "Polyolbion," and at the end of each book he stops to allow his muse to catch her breath. He never allows us to forget what a task he has undertaken.

We sympathize with him as he views the drainage system of the eastern counties.

"By this our little rest, thus having gotten breath
And fairly on our way upon Newmarket heath,
We come upon the ancient ditch expected long
To inspire the muse."

The Chicago drainage canal could not awaken more rapture in a patriotic Illinois bard than did this Newmarket ditch in the sixteenth-century poet. His muse declares it to be "the longest, largest ditch" she had seen in her travels.

At last the vast topographical survey was completed and Drayton took a respectful farewell of his readers.

"Here I this canto end and also therewithal
My England do conclude for which I undertook
This strange herculean task to this my thirtieth book."

With all our liking for geographical expansiveness we have had no poet who took America as seriously as Drayton took England. Perhaps in the Mississippi Valley there may arise a poet who will undertake this strange herculean task.

Alongside of the attempt to emphasize local and national characteristics there is in our present-day poetry an exotic strain. The influence of China and Japan is felt, not only in direct imitation, but by subtle suggestion.

This response to a foreign influence, however, does not make a new school of poetry. It is only a pleasant variation. It is what poets in all ages have done for their own people. There was a period when it was complained that English poetry was "italianated." There was a period when the influence of Persia and Arabia was dominant in the imagination of the Western World. The wonder is that China and Japan have been so long in making their poetical appeal.

It is hardly fair to speak of imitation here. It is rather interpretation, and this has a very great value for us all. We are made to appreciate forms of feeling other than our own. Essential qualities which belong to one culture are communicated in the form of poetry, and become a common possession. The important thing is that the imagery drawn from other lands and alien civilizations makes its appeal to every one.

Vachel Lindsay in the "Chinese Nightingale" introduces us to Chang, a Chinese laundryman in San Francisco, as he lights his joss stick and sees visions out of ancient China. There is a contrast between his prosaic occupation, as he "ironed and ironed, all alone," and the gorgeous orientalism of his imagination.

But it is still more significant that the hard-headed American business man, yielding to the poet's spell, can share Chang's enjoyment; and in doing so there is a rift in the curtain of race that before had seemed so opaque. The same person can enjoy a Vedic hymn, a Hebrew psalm, a Norse war song. A bit of real poetry produced in Greece or China or Czecho-Slovakia or Oklahoma has power to awaken response in persons most distant in point of time and space. So far from appreciating only what corresponds with his own experience the reader often craves that which is altogether different. He is eager for a new sensation. The poetry he most enjoys is not that which he most understands. It is that which does something to him which he cannot understand.

Let us think of a Puritan youth living on Cape Cod in the winter of 1623. The snow is on the ground, the winds are sharp. The boy is not afraid of bears or Indians, but he is afraid of the elders of the church who may come to catechise him. Their faces are stern, their dress is somber, and the east wind has unpleasantly affected their vocal chords. They are good men, but their ways are not alluring. It is Sunday afternoon, and there is only one book which he is allowed to read.

Fortunately he opens upon a bit of pure poetry. It hasn't any moral that he can perceive. It conveys no information. It administers no rebuke. But the words have color and fragrance, and bring a sense of something quite remote from anything in his own experience. There are strings of jewels, and clusters of henna flowers, and myrrh and frankincense, and walled gardens and mountains of spices; there are fountains and flowing streams from Lebanon. And there are dens of lions and "mountains of the leopards." And there are mysterious lovers not reticent after the manner of the Plymouth Plantation, but loudly proclaiming their love to the watchmen that go about the streets. The sense of spring is in the air.

> "My beloved spake, and said unto me,
>   Rise up, my love, my fair one, and come away,
>   For, lo, the winter is past,
>   The rain is over and gone,
>   The flowers appear in the earth,
>   The time of the singing of birds is come."

And with all this beauty there is something

that brings a sudden fear. There are moments
when beauty has a terror.

> "Who is she that looketh forth as the morning,
>   Fair as the moon,
>   Clear as the sun,
>   Terrible as an army with banners?
>   I went down into the garden of nuts
>   To see the green plants of the valley,
>   To see whether the vine budded,
>   And the pomegranates were in flower.
>   Or ever I was aware my soul set me
>   Among the chariots."

What does all this mean? The youthful
Puritan does not know. But he is glad that the
elders of the church had not been able to take all
the poetry out of the Bible.

The modern critic expounds the tenets of the
new school of the Imagists. We listen sym-
pathetically to the doctrine that poetry should
appeal to the senses in a series of vivid images
each one of which is its own excuse for being.
Then we ask, Where is a poem more perfect in
this kind than the ancient "Song of Songs"?
Imagistic poetry is not the only kind, but it is
one kind, and it is very good when it is well done.

The modern poet in his self-conscious moods
may be irritated when he is reminded that the

season's novelties are not so new as he may
have imagined. Fashions of the day are reminiscent of days gone by. But on the other hand in
those happy moments, when with his singing
robes upon him he goes out into the sunshine,
it is a delight to find himself one of an ancient
and honorable company of those whose newness of spirit is perennial. It is a pleasure to him
to think of a reader who, coming for the first
time upon his book, says, "That reminds me."

OUR MOTHER TONGUE

I TAKE for granted that we have a mother tongue, and that it is English. It may please us to speak now and then of the American language, but this little pleasantry does not blind us to the nature of our inheritance. The designation "English" has nothing to do with present-day political or racial distinctions. The most fervent Irish Republican speaks English when he wishes to be understood by his fellow countrymen. The fact that the people in Oklahoma or in South Africa may have idioms unknown to Oxford is immaterial. The English language is what the English-speaking peoples of the earth are making it.

I sympathize with the multitude of teachers who are trying to induce young Americans to honor their mother tongue. They have to meet and overcome all sorts of opposition. In the case of a foreign language, the pupil's mind is without prejudice. If the teacher lays down a rule, it is accepted without question. But in regard to his own language, which he has learned at his mother's knees, he is conservative. The small boy had been speaking the language as long as he can remember, and he is not in the mood to welcome innovations. He is well aware that, if he were to imitate the teacher's peculiarities of speech outside the classroom, he would become an object of the ridicule of his peers. He therefore becomes bilingual.

Language is singularly free from the autocratic sway of the schoolmaster. The usage of the home and the street has far greater authority. Any aberration from this is always looked upon with suspicion. Any strange or unusual expressions drawn from books are tabooed by the young politician with his ear to the ground. Language to him is a means of communication with his fellows, and not a fine art cultivated for art's sake. He does not wish to dazzle or confound his friends, but only to make himself understood in a way that is agreeable to them.

The small boy is essentially right, and the sooner the teacher of English accepts this point of view and improves upon it the better. Language is simply a means of communication between one mind and another. It is a medium for the exchange of thought and feeling. The essential thing is that there should be something to communicate, and that there should be as little waste in the process as possible.

The great difficulty comes when the teacher forgets what language is and treats it as if it were an end in itself. He becomes interested in the vain effort to express accurately and beautifully something that isn't there. Words disconnected with thoughts are like irredeemable paper money.

In pointing out mistakes in popular language, such a teacher does small service if he does not realize that the most correct sentence is a failure if it fails to convey a vivid impression of what was in the speaker's mind. It is not a case where "to be dull is construed to be good."

In an advertisement of a Chiropractors' School I came across this definition of disease:

"Thus you see disease to the chiropractor is not something from the outside that somehow gets inside, but rather it is something (a vibration from the outside) that *cannot* get inside, or something from the inside (a functional impulse) that is imprisoned and cannot reach the outside to which it was sent."

I am not a chiropractor and do not know how far this formula explains the mysteries of pathology, but it seems to be a very good starting-point in the study of language. There are those who are greatly troubled about the foreign influences which get into the language and destroy its native purity.

I think it would be wiser to look into the mind itself for the obstructions to the free flow of ideas. There is something in the mind that cannot get out, and there are impressions from the outside world that cannot get in. The first thing to do is to clear the way. Vigorous thinking and feeling rather than verbal criticism is needed. The thought must have strength enough to break through. There is no language which is good in itself. It is good only when it is a good conductor of ideas. Its one function is to render possible a meeting of minds. An impulse in one mind is translated into a corresponding impulse in another. This may be done through a sentence or through a single word.

It follows that the value of this transfer of thought and emotion depends, not only on the completeness of the process, but on the value of what is transferred. We praise a writer who is perfectly clear, but there are degrees in our admiration. He may express a very limited idea that is in his mind. He does it with admirable lucidity. We see his idea and we see all around it. The transfer is made in a perfectly business-like manner; just as a clerk in a grocery will weigh a pound of tea, and wrap it up neatly and hand it to us over the counter. The transaction is complete. We understand what the person means; and we understand that he does not mean much. In these small and necessary trans-actions verbal accuracy is about all that is re-quired.

But it is different when he struggles with a large and many-sided idea. There has been a conflict in his mind that has not been fully de-cided. He has great hopes and great fears. He wishes to communicate with us and tell us how the battle goes. He tries to tell how his forces are holding out.

These communications are difficult and put a strain upon language. New meanings must be given to familiar words. To give a true account of what is happening in one mind so that it can awaken feeling in another is a great achieve-ment. The power to express a real situation in words is not given to all. Indeed, it is one of the rarest of gifts and therefore one of the most

highly prized. Most of us are painfully in-
articulate. In great crises of life we fall back
on the familiar words which have brought
strength and consolation through many generations. They express what we mean. That is the
function of great literature.

It also expresses all shades of emotion, and all
sorts of reactions — humor, compassion, scorn.
Each has its own vocabulary and its forms of
construction. Only in one's mother tongue can
we recognize and quickly respond to all the
changes which take place in a sensitive mind in
contact with a bewildering situation. So much
can be expressed and suggested. We are in contact not merely with the minds of our contemporaries, but with the accumulated ex-
periences of many generations. Language is a
perpetual surprise. We first get acquainted with
our own thoughts and then we discover their
family resemblance to other people's thoughts.
It is like meeting one's neighbors at a world's
fair. Each is surprised to see the others there as
part of a great cosmopolitan crowd.

I have an idea that had never occurred to me
before, and I am eager to communicate it. But in
my endeavor to express myself I grope around in

my memory for the right word. At last I find it. I have used the word many times, but I have just discovered its meaning. Thousands of persons centuries ago must have made the same distinction that I am making. The man who first used that expression must have had the same experience that I am having.

I want to describe a person for whom I have a great deal of respect. He is mentally alert, morally sound, very intelligent — and yet, what is it that makes him a little wearing — not very, but just a little? There is something that slightly interferes with the pleasure of conversation. He is not overbearing, or bigoted, or fanatical — that would be putting it too strongly. What shall I say? He seems to put an excessive value on his own opinions. Yes, I have the word — *opinionated*.

When we say that a man is opinionated, everybody understands the judgment that is passed upon him. It is not harsh. We all admit that it is a good thing to have clear opinions, and that it is good to make them known. We only mean to state that our friend has the defect of his qualities. He would see this himself and smile good-naturedly at his cock-sureness — if he were not so opinionated.

And cock-sure! The man who first thought of that comparison with the cock must have taken the opinionated man down a peg or two. By the way, that is an idiomatic way of expressing a friendly depreciation. You may think a person should be taken down a peg without wishing him ill. You wouldn't want him to fall to the bottom. And when you come to think about it, depreciate conveys the same idea — *de*=under and *præ-tium*=price. You admit that the article has some value, but you think it ought to be marked down.

And so you might go through the Dictionary. As you thrust your way through the crowd of words, you are continually renewing old acquaintances and making new ones. There are words that smile, and words that smirk, and words that sneer, and words that are like blows. There are coarse, brutal words elbowing and insulting their betters. There are shallow, ambitious words, social climbers trying by vulgar persistence to force their way into good society. There are sly, furtive words with double meanings. Then you will come upon a frank, open-hearted, businesslike word which has but one meaning and doesn't care who knows it. There are shy, beautiful, elusive words which one meets only now and then in out-of-the-way places. There are words that betray their foreign origin which add to the picturesqueness of the scene. Then there are the plain everyday words which we use every day. We could not get along without these day laborers, though we sometimes feel that it is a pity that they should be so sadly overworked.

In dealing with our mother tongue a controversy arises between the eager modernists and those who are lovers of our earlier literature. English is a living language, and is always changing. The idiomatic English of Chaucer's day is not that of the twentieth century. There are some who find difficulty even with the English of the sixteenth century. Is it worth the effort on the part of those who do not aspire to be scholars to read books written for other generations?

I am afraid that those who are scholars have something to answer for in the way they discourage us of the laity from enjoying much that really requires very little effort. When a person reads the commentators on Shakespeare, he is

confounded by the sense of his linguistic in-
competence. So many words seem to have
changed their meanings, and there are so many
allusions that he has not really understood.

But this does not mean that he has not been
able to enjoy Shakespeare; it only means that he
has not had sufficient erudition to enjoy Shake-
spearean scholarship. This will come if he has
time for it. In the mean while Shakespeare is an
open book.

A more serious objection can be made to those
who dismiss writings, witty and wise and spark-
ling, with the epithet "quaint." There is nothing unintelligible or obsolete about them. One
docs not need a glossary to understand them,
only a mind quick enough to enjoy unspoiled
words.

There are very few good sermons that read
well when reduced to print. But one may take
up the sermons of Hugh Latimer and enjoy his
quick thrusts and vivid pictures. How the old
Bible stories fit into the times! It is not that
Latimer's words were quaint; it is that he had a
mastery of our mother tongue. We listen to him
as he preaches to the King:

"Right honorable audience, I will give a history or two that I left out of my last sermon.

"I was in a matter concerning the sturdiness of the Jews, a stiff-necked kind of people; much like our Englishmen nowadays. They liked to break laws and go byways. Howbeit there were some good walkers among them, that walked in the king's highway, ordinarily — plain Dunstable way, and for this I will show you a history from the book of Kings."

After this hearty introduction he goes on with his story:

"King David being in his second childhood had a son named Adonijah. He was a man full of ambition, always climbing, climbing. He was a stout-stomached child. He got him a chariot and men to run before it. Well; algates he would be king. He makes a great feast and he calls Joab, a ring leader of his father's army, a worldly wise man, and one Abiather the chief priest, for it is a marvel if any mischief is at hand, a priest will be at some end of it. They took him as King and they cried, God save King Adonijah."

We see the personages of the conspiracy pass before our eyes, and then we see the sudden collapse of their hopes.

"Then King David said, 'As God liveth Solo-

mon shall be king after me.' And he took and
commanded Nathan and Sadoc to take Solomon
and set him on a mule, and anoint him King.
So they did. And there was such joy and blow-
ing of trumpets that Joab and his company being
in their jollity heard it and suddenly asked, what
is this ado? And when they learned that Solomon was anointed, by and by there was all
whist. All their good cheer was done, and all
that were with Adonijah went away, and let him
reign if he would."

The sermonizers of our day do not tell Bible
stories that way. Their parishioners wish they
could.

What is it that gives the charm to Latimer's
sermon? It is Latimer himself. There he is, a
hearty Englishman with certain religious senti-
ments which he is not ashamed to utter to all
the world. There are very vivid pictures in his
mind, and there is no obstruction between his
mind and ours. The words exactly express what
was in his mind and what now, through their
magic, is in our minds. We walk with him;
"plain Dunstable way."

In judging such language the thought of formal
correctness has no place. The only fitness is the

fitness to the man himself with all his idiosyncrasies. Idiomatic English can be written only by persons who have individual thoughts to communicate.

In the warnings given to the younger generation against slang, I am inclined to the chiropractic philosophy. The evil of slang is not in new words and phrases getting into the language. It lies in their being repeated so often, after their newness has worn off, that they form obstructions to the natural flow of thought.

Indeed, the mother tongue is singularly hospitable to new words. So long as they are used singly, they serve to enrich the language. Even when they are of vulgar origin, they may serve on occasions when no other word would express the exact shade of thought. It is the slang *phrase* that after a few repetitions outlives its usefulness. If it was originally witty, so much the worse for it, for there is nothing more tiresome than wit that has lost the elements of surprise. The habitual use of ready-made phrases tends to reduce the number of ideas that can be vividly expressed. It bears the same relation to language that the old block printing did to printing from movable type.

A sentence or series of sentences could be engraved on wood and a page could thus be printed. But it was a very laborious and expensive process. That particular sequence of letters would not answer for the other pages of the book.

By the invention of movable type printing became an effective means for the diffusion of ideas. With twenty-six letters all sorts of combinations could be made. After one printing the type could be distributed and then recombined.

With a stock of clear-cut words, which are capable of being combined in any number of ways, we are able to express all sorts of thoughts as they arise in our minds. There are possibilities of surprise. The same word differently combined with others produces effects which delight us. Language becomes a living thing yielding itself at every moment to a fresh impulse of the mind.

Any phrase repeated too often becomes an obstruction to the flow of thought and feeling. It forms a clot.

Shakespeare speaks of "the witching hour of night." It is a good phrase, but he does not repeat it. Milton writes:

"They trip it as they go
On the light fantastic toe."

It serves his purpose, but it is not made a synonym for the word "dance." But the young man
who writes of the party at Squire Higgin's says:
"The young folks tripped the light fantastic till
long after the witching hour." And the chances
are that in his account of the next party he will
fall into the same Shakespeare-Milton combination of words, which in his mind is now indi-
visible.

The study of fatigue has been carried on, not
only in relation to living beings, but into the in-
animate world, and we hear of the fatigue of
metals. A New England granite dealer told
me that Southern granite is stronger than the
Northern. He attributed this to the fact that the
Northern granite, while still strong enough for
all practical purposes, had been more or less
fatigued by its struggle for existence during the
glacial period. In Georgia these stresses had been
avoided and the granite retained a more youthful quality. The fatigue of words deserves a
special study.

Words that are unequally yoked together are
apt to lose their individuality. When there is

incompatibility of temper between an adjective and a noun, and they are not allowed to separate, they both lead a drab existence. The recognition of the right of each word to be itself, is one of the first conditions of good writing. All words expressive of admiration or reprobation are apt to lose their meaning. "Unspeakable Turk" expresses nothing but an inherited antipathy. By applying the epithet to some other nation it might be restored to its original strength. There is no objection to a young girl saying "terribly nice" if it seems to her amusing. There is something pleasantly humorous in the incongruous combination of adjectives. The person who first thought of it must have chuckled over it. The objection to it comes when it is used by somebody who doesn't think of it as amusing.

The emphasis on the teaching of the mother tongue is justified by the fact that language is something more than a tool of thought. It is a part of the very process of thinking. Our ideas are clarified in the very attempt to express them. In the effort to communicate them to others we make them more intelligible to ourselves.

HISTORY FOR THE AGEING

THE lessons of history are for all periods of life, and historians are becoming mindful of the fact. Mr. H. G. Wells has written a History of the World that appeals to the young reformer who is filled with a sense of exuberant moral vigor, but who is afraid that he may have been born too late for its exercise. What if all the great battles have been fought and the heroic age is passed? Mr. Wells reassures him. By a rapid survey of the history of mankind he shows him that everything has been leading up to the exciting predicament in which we find ourselves at the moment of going to press. The newcomer can plunge into the fray with the assurance that he has come upon the scene in the very nick of time.

Mr. Van Loon has been writing history for the benefit of the very young. By means of simple illustrations he has made history intelligible to a child who can read and enjoy pictures. As for the aged, they have always had histories adapted to a reminiscent mood, where "all the angles of the strife are rounded into calm."

But there is one class that has not been sufficiently cared for. I am thinking, not of the aged, but of the ageing. There is a period when a person becomes conscious that he is not quite so young as he once was. There is a slight consciousness of moral fatigue. He is not ready to give up the struggle, but he sometimes wonders whether it is worth the effort. There is a faint suspicion of futility. He is rather more critical of others than he used to be, and at the same time less confident of his own ability to improve them. In regard to large public questions he is more apt to take gloomy views. He begins to view with alarm movements which used to excite his curiosity. He observes that there is a younger generation which is inclined to be obstreperous. When he hears prognostications of the utter collapse of civilization, he hopes that it may not come in his day, but he sees no way to prevent it.

At this period, the lessons of history seem to confirm him in a fatalistic attitude. The predestinarian theologian, who declares that what is to be, will be, may be argued against, but there is no getting away from the historian when he points out the fact that what has been, has been. It can be proved that every event has had its antecedent causes. History, as a record of things that have happened, bears a stern aspect of inevitability. They happened in spite of the efforts of men to make them turn out differently. If that is what history teaches, why should we disquiet ourselves in vain in the attempt to direct our destiny?

Just here is an opportunity for the historian who loves his fellow men to be of service. Let him write history for the benefit of the ageing. He should aim to rescue the faint-hearted reader from fatalism.

The history I have in mind should be the history of what never happened. It should be the history of catastrophes which were greatly feared in their day and believed to be inevitable. The wise and prudent saw them written in the Book of Fate, and the timid accepted them as accomplished facts. But somehow the prognostications failed. The things which were foretold with such distinctness never came to pass.

Why did they not come to pass? That is something for the historian to find out and explain to us. If the historian of actual events finds it necessary to show us the cause of what happened, the historian of Fears and Phobias should explain why so many things which seemed so real to the imaginative, and so logical to the intelligent, never took place. Such investigation may lead him far. It might be supposed that the historian of what never happened might have difficulty in collecting documentary material. On the contrary, there is a vast literature which he can draw upon. He has no difficulty in getting at original sources.

When one is trying to find out what actually took place at a critical period, he is surprised at the meagerness of the evidence at hand. But if he wishes to know what people at the time thought was taking place, he has ample evidence. Everybody was talking about it. Eager intellectuals were explaining it; that it did not happen at all is something that may not have been discovered till a generation after. In the mean time it has its interest and importance for every student of human nature.

An instructive history might be written of the great Jesuit plot for the destruction of Protestant England, and the invasion and conquest of the island by the vast armies carried across the Channel. It was to be followed by the setting up of the Spanish Inquisition and the confiscation of the property of English gentlemen. This melancholy history covers the period from the time of Elizabeth to the reign of George III. The historian should tell us why Englishmen were in such a panic. He should also explain the futility of the plots and counter plots. There should be a chapter on the innocent victims of Fear.

A history of the destruction of the American Republic through the machinations of a military oligarchy known as "The Society of the Cincinnati" would be highly instructive. There is a great amount of literary material, for the conspiracy aroused intense public interest, and its details were well known to the general public, though concealed from the conspirators.

It was in 1783 that certain officers of the American Army met and passed the following ominous resolution:

"The officers of the American Army possess high veneration for the character of the illustrious Roman, Lucius Quintus Cincinnatus, and, resolved to follow his example, they with propriety denominate themselves The Society of the Cincinnati."

To one familiar with ancient history the plot

is clear. Cincinnatus is the great name used to
deceive the unthinking plebeians of the newly
liberated States. All they know about him is
that which has been told them. Cincinnatus returned to the plough. It is a fine gesture and
endears him to simple-minded agriculturists.
But how easy it is to beat a ploughshare into a
sword. The Society of the Cincinnati is to be
hereditary, and we all know what that means.
History is full of the records of greedy nobles
who, gaining the confidence of the people in a
war of liberation, build up great families on the
ruins of the Commonwealth. Let a contemporary tell the story:

"The order of the Cincinnati is the creation of
a military nobility. It will, in the course of time,
incorporate itself in the constitution and utterly
destroy it. If this be doubted let us appeal to
history and trace the origin and progress of similar institutions. The same causes will produce
the same effects. The next generation of the
Cincinnati will be the nobles. In less than a century there will be a line of separation between
the descendants of the Cincinnati and their fellow citizens. There will be two classes, the patri-
cians and the plebeians. Numerous, warlike,

superior to all the rest, superior to the laws, what shall protect the people from the despotic rule of the Cincinnati?"

In vain did Washington argue that the officers who formed the society were honest republicans who, having saved their country, had no desire to enslave it. History taught that all prospective tyrants talked that way. The existence of the society was a threat which chilled the blood of the far-seeing. Newspapers and pamphlets gave the country ample warning of its doom.

But when I was asked, a number of years ago, to address a chapter of the Society of the Cincinnati, I was surprised at the amiable appearance of the gentlemen before me. Time had done its ameliorating work and taken away all evidence of the will to rule. The descendants of these Revolutionary officers could not be distinguished from the descendants of men of the ranks. Most of them were not even military men. Their demeanor was altogether peaceful.

It is evident that if ever the Cincinnati were a menace, the time has long since passed. Indeed, there is not the least evidence to show that anything ever happened to justify the alarm they created in their early days. The historian should

tell us why the society did not develop into a
military aristocracy, and why its members did
not want to do anything of the kind. Investigation of this matter might throw some light on
American character.

A history of the Jacobin revolution in America about the year 1787, and culminating in 1800
in the overthrow of constitutional government
by Thomas Jefferson, has the possibility of much
thrilling description. The reign of terror has
been vividly prognosticated by many excellent
Federalists. That the horrors that they describe
never took place is one of the curious accidents
of history. They were logically involved in the
great revolutionary movement.

The history of the French Revolution in
France has often been told. But the history of
the French Revolution in England and America
requires philosophic treatment. That thousands
of people believed in it is a matter that cannot
be doubted any more than that multitudes of
people at the present time believe in the possibility of a Bolshevist revolution in America.
What happened in one place is easily attributed
to another.

Did not Jacobins in Philadelphia wear liberty caps and rejoice over the execution of Louis XVI? Were there not frontiersmen in Kentucky who were ready to repeat the orgies of the Parisian mobs? And did not Thomas Jefferson say, "A little rebellion now and then is good for the country"? Was there not ample reason for the Alien and Sedition Laws to keep the revolutionary pestilence out of the country?

A study of the state of mind induced by a violent revolution in one country, upon the law-abiding people of another, would lead to a consideration of what a revolution is and how it is propagated. In order to answer such questions, one must distinguish between those rapid changes of opinion which take place among the masses of the people, and which lead to new political and social organizations, and those sudden and violent upheavals which are accompanied by mob fury and the mad impulse to destroy life and property. One is a revolution in thought which may be carried out in an orderly fashion. The other is a terrible catastrophe. The tendency is to look upon the two things as though they were identical. To the amazed lookers-on, the French Revolution was but another name for the Terror.

A revolutionary thought may spread from one country to another. But a revolution in the sense of a violent and destructive upheaval, does not spread. It is futile to treat it as though it were a pestilence and could be checked by a rigid quarantine. It is an earthquake due to the dislocation of underlying strata. In the vicinity of the fracture there is destruction, and everything is shaken, but earthquakes are not catching.

The causes of what happened in France after the falling of the Bastille, and what happened in Russia after the deposition of the Czar, must be sought in France and in Russia. The local causes account for the events. Each people has its own grievances, and is driven to violent action when they become intolerable and there seems to be an opportunity for relief. But where these causes do not exist, the catastrophe does not occur. The history of the violent revolutions that have not happened amply proves the truth of this observation.

The history of the secession movement in America is instructive as to the relation between political theory and what actually happens.

The historian of events is likely to give the impression that this relation is much simpler than it actually is. There actually was a war between the States. The Southern States insisted that each sovereign State had, under the Constitution, a right to withdraw from the Union. The Northern States denied this right, and resisted the attempt to set up another government. In the light of the events which took place in the sixties, the history of States' Rights doctrine in the South is given great emphasis. It seems inevitable that what had been theoretically proclaimed as right should have been attempted by the force of arms.

But did the devotion to the doctrine of States' Rights determine the fact that the South should be the section that should venture to secede? The history of threatened secessions that never happened should not be neglected.

That there was danger of the States falling apart was seen from the time of the first Confederation. But the logical line of cleavage seemed to be, not that between the North and the South, but between the East and the West. The ridge of the Alleghanies seemed to furnish a strategic frontier. And the difference in temperament between the men on the seacoast and those who had crossed the mountains seemed to make the danger more acute.

Hardly had the government been established when the fear of disunion was manifest. An independent observer from beyond the mountains writes:

"We can raise twenty thousand troops this side of the mountains. Preparations are now making to drive out the Spaniards from the mouth of the Mississippi. If we are not countenanced by the United States, our allegiance will be thrown off and some other power applied to receive and support us. You are as ignorant of this country as Great Britain was of America."

That this was not an unreal danger, the story of Burr's conspiracy proves to us. But what about the secession movement in New England? So late as the Hartford Convention in 1814, it was believed that it was possible for the Northeastern States to set up a government of their own. The Federalist leaders had despaired of the Republic, and they were cautiously discussing what means should be taken in the event of a new emergency. A newspaper poet expresses the popular feeling about the Convention:

"These states ought not united stand;
    The Western and the Southern
Too strong have grown for New England
    Or those we call the Northern.

"A separation to effect
    Long have we all been striving,
And soon to gain it we expect,
    Our cause we think looks thriving.

"For Massachusetts strong has made
    An open declaration
She's ready now to take the lead
    And force a separation.

"The Boston folks, a people wise,
    Religious, firm, and steady,
In opposition first shall rise
    And we must all be ready."

Here was the first rumbling of a storm. What
became of the storm? It passed around. The
secession of New England belongs to the History
of What Never Happened. The Hartford Convention turned out to be a harmless affair after
all.

"We took a trip to Hartford, Jim
    Thought all the Feds would join
In separation of the States
    As Henry did divine.

Strong's eastern wise men did go on
    To Washington also,
But horrid fates befell these babes,
    Jim Madison, my jo.

But wherever the split might come, along the
line of the Hudson, or along the ridge of the Alleghanies, the wise and the prudent were agreed
that there was no power in the Union which
could coerce the States. De Tocqueville summed
up the situation: "Patriotism is directed to the
State. If the sovereignty of the Union were to
engage in a struggle with the States, its defeat
may be confidently predicted."

This appeared to be capable of mathematical
demonstration. "The increase of the number of
States weakens the tie which holds them together. At the end of the century there will be
a hundred millions of people divided into forty
States. I shall refuse to believe in the duration
of a government, spread over a country equal to
half of Europe to avoid all rivalry, ambitions,
and struggles between them, and to direct their
independent activities to the accomplishment of
one design."

Why did not all this happen which was so
clearly foreseen? What were the incalculable elements which were involved?

The history of the agrarian revolt in the United States cuts a great figure in the minds of perturbed patriots with a classical education. Of course it happened in the time of Tiberius Gracchus, and afterwards in the Peasants' Revolt in the sixteenth century. Demagogues fostered the discontents of the peasant proprietors and made no end of trouble for the government. About 1835 this movement came to a head and threatened the existence of the Republic. The newspapers of the day are full of the direful warnings against the dreadful doings of the Loco-focos. Who were the Loco-focos?

"Agrarian," says von Holst, "was the accursed name fastened on them to make them the abomination of all who took an interest in law and order. Care was taken not to define the horrible idea too accurately — a monstrous, socialistic, communistic something."

The American farmer from the time of Shays's rebellion in Worcester County, Massachusetts, to the time of the Non-partisan League in North Dakota, has manifested a very genius for making himself misunderstood. He has had his grievances, high taxes, mortgages, excessive transportation charges, and the like. But when he has tried to express himself, that "socialistic, communistic something" has emerged out of the ancient history books. Agrarian' revolts have happened in the past and they have been very dreadful. In times of political excitement the American farmer is suspected of a desire to arise in the night and cut his own throat after having divided his own land among the proletariat. The Kansan agriculturist, when he declaims against "Wall Street," is supposed to be infected with Bolshevism.

The History of the Know-Nothing Party would be instructive. It would tell of the great feud between the Protestant and the Catholic. It would describe how the native Americans rose in their wrath to drive out the intruders, by a combination of a secret society and an open political party. There is no lack of passionate invective and dire foreboding. But why did not more come of it? What has prevented similiar movements from going beyond a certain stage? There are always people ready to kindle racial and religious animosities. Why have they not been more successful? These people must have troubles of their own. Perhaps our system of public education is more successful than we realize, and feuds have here a tendency to die out. The historian of phobias should look into this.

From the fact that so many of the things which people have most dreaded have never happened, let no one draw the conclusion that the fears were groundless, and that everything would have turned out for the best anyway. This is to fall into the very fatalism from which we seek to escape. The dangers were real, though the fears may have been exaggerated.

If so many evils which were foreseen were averted, it indicates that the efforts of wise and good men have not been futile. There is no need to yield to a threat. The forces of order are stronger than in our moments of depression we are able to think. If a free society has a tendency to right itself, it is because there are multitudes of right-minded citizens who can be counted upon to do the right thing in an emergency. Civilization has a reserve force that no one of us is able to estimate properly, and until the reserves are exhausted there is no reason to give up hope.

The historian of What Never Happened can deliver his ageing reader from the notion that all

that is threatened is sure to come to pass. When
he is asked to yield to the inevitable, he should
learn that procrastination may sometimes be a
virtue. By delaying the yielding, the aspect of
inevitability may fade away. Among other
things he may be delivered from the tyranny of
the scientific prognosticators whose knowledge
of the machinery of civilization is greater than
their faith in the power of man to control it.
One is reminded when reading the forecasts of
these learned but low-spirited gentlemen of the
remarks of Rollo on his first voyage on a steamboat.

His father had elaborately explained the
mechanism of the steam engine and the lesson
had been thoroughly learned. A fog arose and
the steamer anchored, while a small boat was
sent out to make sure of its location. Before the
boat returned the fog lifted and the captain gave
orders to get up steam.

"Father," said Rollo, looking a little alarmed,
"then the steamboat will go off and leave the
little boat behind."

"No!" said his father.

"Why, yes, father," said Rollo, "the steam
will crowd into the cylinder first above the piston

and then below so as to make it move up and down, and the piston will drive the beam, and the beam the crank, and the crank the paddle wheels, and the paddle wheels will carry the boat, along through the water. I think they had better not fire up till they are ready to go."

"No," replied his father, "they will not let the steam get into the cylinder."

"How can they help it?" said Rollo.

Then his father explained that there was a stop-cock, which when turned, prevented the steam from escaping from the boiler into the cylinder.

"Then the steam will have to stay in the boiler, and it will keep on increasing till the boiler will burst," said Rollo.

Then his father explained that there was a safety valve which let off the surplus steam.

"Is there?" said Rollo.

"Yes," replied his father.

"That's a good plan," said Rollo, "I'm glad of that."

The knowledge of the mechanism of society and of the forces behind it needs to be supplemented by a knowledge of the various contrivances for bringing them under human control.

They are not perfect, but it is remarkable how many explosions they prevent. When we study the safety devices which the wit of man has invented we may join with Rollo in his discreet expression of approbation of what has already been accomplished.

INSTITUTIONS AND OPINIONS

THE great writers of our own age are, we have reason to suppose, the companions and forerunners of some unimagined change in our social condition or the opinions which cement it. The cloud of mind is discharging its collected lightning, and the equilibrium between institutions and opinions is now restoring or is about to be restored.

Shelley, in his Preface to *Prometheus Unbound.*

SHELLEY'S expectation of a sudden revolution that would restore the equilibrium between institutions and opinions is based upon an idea which is held both by the ardent revolutionist and the stubborn conservative. They both act upon a certain conception of "normalcy." There is, they assume, a normal equilibrium between institutions and opinions. The institution is the embodiment of certain opinions that are held by the people. Any change in opinion disturbs the natural balance, and a violent revolution is likely to follow.

The man of conservative temper dreads this disaster. He takes for granted that the institutions and opinions which he inherited are normal. They are accepted by him as a part of the order of nature, and he is disturbed when they are questioned by other minds. It is not that he objects to freedom of thought in itself. What he fears are its consequences to the institution to which he is loyal, and of whose usefulness he is assured. He is fearful of a change of opinion, which he looks upon as a form of social disintegration.

The radical idealist, starting from the same assumption, welcomes new thought because it is destructive of an order of things which he believes should be destroyed. When new opinions have overthrown the archaic institutions, they will create new institutions in harmony with themselves. He is inclined to be very literal in his description of the new order, comparing it with the pattern which is in his own mind. He sees it in its entirety and all very good.

But is this fundamental assumption warranted? Granted that there is some relation between institutions and opinions, is it so simple as the eager revolutionist or the anxious conservative imagines? Is the normal and healthy condition one in which people are genially uncritical of their own institutions and undesirous of changing them? Does radical thinking lead necessarily or even usually to violent revolution? On the other hand, does violent revolution lead to a state of things that permanently satisfies the advanced thinker? At what historical period would we look as an example of a complete equilibrium between opinions and institutions?

I cannot recall any period in which the best thinkers expressed satisfaction with the institutions of their own time. Always "the cloud of mind is discharging its collected lightning." Sometimes the storm is more intense and the flashes more frequent, but it is always going on. Where was a prophet who was satisfied with the institutions of religion as they existed in his own time? His message is continually, "I will overturn, and overturn, and overturn till he whose right it is shall come." Where was an educator who was not a keen critic of the schools? Where was a great jurist who was satisfied with all the procedure of the courts? What hard things Washington said about the organization of his army! How bitter is your successful captain of industry in his denunciation of the waste permitted by industrial organizations! Even in regard to that most ancient institution, the family, it is the enlightened parent who finds most fault.

This is not accidental. It is involved in the

real relation of thought to institutions. An institution does not exist because it expresses, in any exact way, our opinions. We may have our opinions about it which may be more or less unfavorable, and yet we may belong to it and have a part in its upbuilding. The taxpayer grumbles, but he pays. The unwilling schoolboy is an essential part of the school. At the town meeting there is always the chronic objector, who opposes every popular measure.

The greater institutions which engage the attention of the historian of civilization, and to which he gives names, seem to grow up without much planning. They do not represent a consensus of opinion, but are the result of a series of circumstances, and the reactions which result from them. The necessities of vast numbers of people force certain modes of action.

There is one phrase which expresses the relation of an individual to the institutional life of which he is a part. We say, "We are all in the same boat." Now, it does not matter how we got into the boat, or what is our opinion of the voyage. The one essential point is that we are all in the same predicament. So long as we are in the boat, we have to make the best of one another. That we may prefer another boat and other passengers makes not the slightest difference. Here we are and here is the boat, such as it is. Self-preservation demands a certain amount of public spirit.

The great basic institutions are of this nature. We do not voluntarily join them; we find ourselves in them. Only a few people change their nationality, and even they seldom do it from a preference for one form of government over another. The people living in the same territory find themselves subject to the same laws and expected to perform certain patriotic duties. To expect them to have identical opinions is to mistake the nature of thought and the nature of nationality.

Among the persons at the present time inhabiting the territory of the United States and subject to its laws, there are, I suppose, advocates of every political theory and economic heresy known to man. Among them are many which, if carried out to their logical conclusions, would be fatal to the existence of republican institutions. If inquisition were made, it would be found that many of these subversive principles are held by the native-born as well as by those who have come from other lands. When we have defined what we consider the true American doctrine, we find many American citizens who do not conform to our standard.

There are those who in their anxiety for the welfare of the country and the purity of its institutions would set up a Holy American Inquisition to root out political heresy. But every attempt to bring about such homogeneity by forcible means must defeat its own purpose. It only reveals the actual diversity which exists.

We come back to the boat. In this case, the boat is the territory which we inhabit. Here we are, members of the Ku-Klux-Klan, Knights of Columbus, members of various Chambers of Commerce, Hebrews, Anti-Semites, Socialists, Semi-Socialists, farmers, labor leaders, and old-line Republicans. The one thing we have in common is the place where we live. Unless we intend to kill each other off, we must learn to inhabit this territory peaceably. Our laws and institutions were invented for this very purpose. We are all in the same predicament. We must protect our neighbor's rights if we are to expect him to protect ours.

One of the rights which we value very highly

is the right to express our own minds. When this right is exercised freely by all members of the community, there will be much contention and many foolish and bitter things will be said. The most sacred institutions will be criticized, and an outsider might suppose that they were in danger of destruction. But to the believer in free government, all this is not only natural, but highly encouraging. Our political institutions are designed for this very purpose — to allow the largest number of people, living in a given territory, to express themselves fully and freely. So long as they keep the peace, the law looks upon their diversities of opinion with an indulgent eye. The safety of the State lies in the fact that extreme views, when they are allowed free expression, tend to neutralize each other. The common sense of the crowd is a more moderating force than any censorship.

As to religious institutions, the territorial consideration is no longer important. We have given up the ancient idea that the inhabitants of a particular region must all belong to the same church. But there are many who insist that for that very reason each church must formulate a body of opinions to be held by all its members.

When any one comes to disagree with these formulations, he should either hold his peace, or give up his membership. Any full and frank discussions from within the body would thus become impossible. Intellectual conformity would become the test of loyalty. It is an automatic method for driving thinkers out of the Church. And yet the Church needs thinkers.

But why should uniformity of opinion be looked upon as essential to a church, any more than to a family? Why should not people who hold a variety of opinions still feel their need of one another, and unite heartily in order to improve their spiritual condition? Religion organizes itself in response to human needs rather than in assent to any formulated opinion. It defines itself in deeds rather than in words.

"The disciples were called Christians first at Antioch." Before that they were spoken of as people of "the way." We are told that "there arose no small stir about that way." Of course it was not so much the way as the fact that there were people who actually walked in it that caused the stir. It didn't matter that they had not yet agreed upon any name; they were recognized by the way they actually lived.

One wonders whether much would have been lost if the movement had been allowed to go on in that manner. Perhaps it has gone on in that manner more than we realize. The great ecclesiastical personages whose names loom so large in church history had often very little to do with the obscure people of the way, except to try to repress them when they became too troublesome. Yet the Church has survived because these people have always persevered, and have refused to be driven out of the institution which belonged to them.

In times when there is no small stir in the Church, and much dissatisfaction with its forms of worship and of thought, it is not safe to jump to the conclusion that the Church is going to pieces. It may be that those are signs of a new awakening. An institution that sets out to reform the world must from time to time reform itself. It may be now as when Paul and Silas came to Thessalonica, and it was rumored that they "that turn the world upside down are come hither also."

Of course Paul and Silas did not actually turn the world upside down, desperately as they tried to do it, — and neither have their successors.

After centuries of Christian endeavor a citizen of the Roman Empire would find much that was familiar in London or New York. But the essential thing is that the people who try to turn the selfish and brutal world upside down are still working. They are not discouraged, and all attempts to exterminate them have failed.

Their protests against existing wrongs and popular superstitions are still heard. The play of spiritual forces upon actual conditions still goes on. Once the critics of social institutions were looked upon as enemies of society. Now it is coming to be seen that they have a function that is creative. That society is in the healthiest condition, and has the best promise of long life, which produces the greatest number of free and virile individuals who are not satisfied with it as it is, and who are eagerly and intelligently endeavoring to transform it into something better. Such a society will be the scene of many conflicts of opinion, and it will thrive on them. It will develop unevenly. It will organize itself according to needs and not according to doctrines. Its growth will be illogical and unpredictable. It will not correspond to any man's idea of Utopia. Unlike Utopia it will be interesting.

THE CONSERVATISM
OF GUIDE-POSTS

In considering the relations of opinions to institutions, there is a third element which must be taken into account — the formulations of opinions that are no longer held. That is to say, the *opinion* is no longer held, but the form of words which expressed it is held, and that very tenaciously. The formula has a way of surviving long after it has severed its connection with its original meaning. These ghosts of old opinions haunt their former dwelling-places.

It is often much harder to change the name of a familiar institution than it is to change its actual character. The consequence is that we are confused by many misnomers. I have been struck by the conservatism of guide-posts. Their prime function is to point the way to travelers, and one might suppose that they would be kept strictly up-to-date. Their didactic purpose is so evident, they have so few words at their disposal, and there is such obvious necessity to preserve a reputation for veracity, that there would seem to be no occasion for historical romanticism. Yet as a matter of fact they have a tendency to forget the facts of the present in their fond recollection of the past.

At a fork in the road with which I have long been pleasantly familiar, there stood till recently a guide-post which bore the inscription, "Tamworth I. W. 2 miles."

Years ago, when I first passed that way, I inquired of a local loiterer, "What does the I. W. stand for?"

"Iron Works."

"Where are the Iron Works?"

My laconic friend pointed, not to the road, but to the guide-post, and, as if teaching a child a lesson on the blackboard, repeated slowly:

"Tamworth Iron Works, Two Miles."

But my desire for knowledge was more realistic than literary, and leaving the letter of the board I tried to get at the facts.

"Are there any iron works there?"

"No! not to say iron-*works*. But Chocorua village used to be called the Iron Works. They say there were iron works there in 1812. Must have burned down about that time. If it's Chocorua village you want to go to, that's the road."

For more than a century the guide-post had stood at the parting of the ways, pointing its slow, unmoving finger toward iron works that had ceased to exist. A hundred years is a long time, and the boards must have been renewed many times, but always with the same misinformation.

Now that a radical change has been made and the "I. W." has been dropped, the same conservative tendency is seen on the other arm of the guide-post, that points northward. I read the familiar information — "Piper House 5 miles." Now of my own knowledge I can testify that the Piper House changed hands a dozen years ago and the new proprietor gave it a new name. The traveler going five miles will see no sign of the Piper House. That name is one with Nineveh and Tyre. But doubtless it will remain on the guide-post for the next quarter of a century.

In Harvard Square in Cambridge there is an old milestone that declares that it is "8 miles to Boston." No one has disturbed it, though any one who walks to Boston Common would not need to travel half the distance that is alleged. When the stone was placed in position a century and a half ago, the traveler had to go around through Roxbury. That more direct access has long since been given to the city makes no difference to the milestone.

The conservatism of guide-boards may be confusing to strangers and irritating to persons of a logical mind, but after all it is consistent with a great deal of real progressiveness. We must distinguish between four elements — the road, the guide-board, the people who customarily use the road, and the people who pay any serious attention to the guide-board.

So far as the road is concerned, it has made very little difference what the guide-board has said. It has gone on its stubborn way up hill and down as becomes a New Hampshire highway. And the people who have customarily used it for the last century have never been misled by the guide-post, for they have paid little attention to it. They knew where they were going and that was sufficient. It was only the occasional stranger who was ever confused, for he was the only one who ever paid serious attention to the words of direction.

I think that this accounts for those anomalies which are found in all long-established institutions. They remain because the people who belong to the institution are not seriously inconvenienced by them. An organization starts out to do one thing and gradually comes to do another. It changes its purpose, but not its statement of purpose. Everybody who belongs to it knows what it is doing and judges it accordingly. It is like a railroad system which has expanded till what was once the main line is only a branch.

No church which was considering only those who were brought up within its own fold would think it necessary to revise its formularies. It would be much easier to reinterpret them. By retaining the old words and giving them new meanings, progress goes on without a jolt. There may be many articles which are treated like silent letters in a familiar word. We do not sound them, but there would be something queer in the look of the page if they were not there.

The call for revision comes when the appeal is made to strangers, who have no associations with the words and therefore take them literally. What, they ask, does this institution really stand for to-day? In the attempt to answer the aims, purposes, and beliefs have to be restated in the language of to-day.

No political party would revise its platform if

it were not thinking of the new voters and how to win them. It would much prefer to reaffirm loyalty to the platform of four years ago, and to point proudly to the fact that not a syllable had been changed.

Whenever an institution is seriously engaged in revising its familiar formulas in the interest of greater clearness, we may be sure that it is alive. It is desirous of making converts and to that end it must make itself understood.

THE LABORATORY METHOD
IN MORALS

SOCRATES has so long been received in good society that it is hard to do justice to the Athenians of his day who looked upon him as a dangerous character. We forget the verdict against him that he was a corrupter of youth. Had he confined his conversation to his coevals, and sat down with elderly gentlemen to discuss the nature of virtue, no objection could have been made because no harm could be done to their well-seasoned intelligences.

But Socrates sought out young men and put questions to them. And then he didn't furnish them with any ready-made answers, but incited them to ask more questions. Moreover, they were questions of the most practical kind which had to do with conduct. Soon everything was unsettled. Young Athens, instead of listening gravely to its elders, was asking, Why? The guardians of order were alarmed. Surely there were some things that ought to be taken for granted — at least by the young. Socrates should be given a dose of hemlock, then Youth would be safe.

It will not do to say that this was a false alarm, and that Socrates was really a safe person. There was a reason for the anxiety that was felt in regard to him. Some of his pupils turned out badly and made no end of trouble for the State. Respectable people couldn't forget Alcibiades.

It is all very well to say that we should test everything, and accept nothing that we do not find to be reasonable. But what if the thing to be hazarded in the test is your own life? You have only one life to experiment with. If you make a fatal mistake, other people may learn a lesson from it, but you cannot. Here is a substance which excites your curiosity. It is labeled poison. But is it? How shall you find out? Taste it and see. Yes, but if you taste it and it is poison, you can't see.

It is the shortness of life, the inexorableness of the consequences of mistake, that make the experimental method seem inapplicable in the realm of morals. To learn by our own blunders, implies that time will be given us for another trial. But the cruel fact is that opportunities come to us that are never repeated. Following a sudden impulse, it is possible for the youth to do an act which determines his whole life, and from whose consequences he can never escape, however bitterly he may repent.

Moreover, the moral questions propounded by Socrates were, after all, much simpler than those which confront the inquiring youth of to-day. It was more possible for the unassisted mind to grapple with the problems presented. The scope of inquiry was more restricted. If one went astray, he was not likely to get so completely bewildered as in the intricacies of modern thinking.

The youth of to-day finds himself a part of a highly organized social order. The customs he is asked to obey have been the results of many causes, through long periods of evolution. Some of them are doubtless only the survivals of primitive taboos; others are the result of costly experience. They represent laws which cannot be transgressed with impunity. He is confronted with many a stern "Thou Shalt Not." What does the prohibition mean? Perhaps there is an excellent reason. "There is a way that seemeth good to a man, but the end thereof is death." But on the other hand there are ways that seem dangerous to timid souls which are only the ways of the expanding life. Shall he decline the adventure? To know the world one must not think to escape all perils.

Before one turns away from the experimental method in morals, he should take a lesson from those who have carried it farthest, and made it yield its finest fruits. It is by the methods approved by physical science that moral science may be improved.

We speak of the laboratory method as that of ceaseless experimentation. It is that, but it is something more. It is experiment made with due regard to the personal safety of the experimenter. The laboratory is a place where people are dealing with the most dangerous things, and getting the maximum of knowledge with the least waste and the smallest risk of disaster.

Under laboratory conditions the most deadly bacillus is studied, its life history is made known, it is allowed to multiply in a culture medium adapted to it, but it is not allowed to escape and destroy the observer. In order to study rabies, one does not have to be bitten by a mad dog. In the chemical laboratories everything is open to test. High explosives are handled. Nobody accepts a mere tradition concerning them. But the tests are made in quantities, and under conditions that have been determined by considerations of safety. No one proposes to blow up the laboratory as an experiment.

When youth with disconcerting seriousness begins to ask fundamental questions in regard to sex, property, or religion, it should be met with a candor equal to its own. When it asks for the truth, it should not be given the half truth. When it asks the reason why of any social custom, it should be encouraged to persevere until it finds the real reason.

When the young man says for the first time, "I am the captain of my soul," it is not the time to preach childish acquiescence. When he takes command of his own ship, he is not in the mood to tolerate interference. But his assertion of independence need have in it no trace of bravado. Because he is captain is no reason for him to tear up his charts and run his ship on the rocks. There is such a thing as a science of navigation, and it is his business to understand it.

In newly emancipated minds the danger comes, not so much from independent judgment, as from carelessness in making experiments or in too great docility in listening to the advice that is offered. In seeking the knowledge necessary to the guidance of life, too much is taken for granted without being tested.

It is because they do not take their independent commands seriously enough that so many make shipwreck. Let us take, for example, the moral questions relating to sex. Nowhere has there been such insistent demands for independence in judgment. We are told that there has been a "conspiracy of silence" in regard to one of the most important parts of life. The blight of Puritanism with its inhibitions and its repressions is upon us. We are victims of ancient taboos. The only escape is through fuller knowledge and a frank facing of realities.

To this we readily agree, if the whole matter be treated with the high seriousness which it deserves. But how shall that necessary knowledge be obtained? How shall we test the customs that have come down to us, and distinguish between a meaningless taboo and the wisdom of experience? How shall we draw the line between personal liberty and our duty to the social order?

Immediately a host of imaginative and emotional writers, who have emancipated themselves from conventionality, offer their services. The old reticences are cast aside. They declare themselves ready to break the conspiracy of silence in the name of literary art.

But are these guides competent? Is there any way by which they may be tested? Is it to a work of fiction that we go when we are seriously seeking facts? There is something rather incongruous in seeing people start to investigate an exceedingly complicated problem, and end with a discussion of a daring novel or a much-talked-of photo play.

One soon discovers that many of the modern pleas for greater freedom in the treatment of the problems of sex are not made in behalf of more thorough scientific investigation, but rather in behalf of the literary artist. The appeal is for more imagination and emotion, and not for more rigid inquiry into reality. Morality is identified with conventionality. It is treated as if it were merely the concern of the commonplace individual, and is supposed to be in a precarious condition in the case of the "young person" who is to be shielded from the rude contact with reality. On the other hand, Art is supposed to be the mysterious liberator. Genius is a law unto itself and makes its own standards. "To the pure all things are pure," and to the artistic judgment that which shocks the mediocre notions of propriety is admirable.

This distinction between an artistic and a moral judgment is an important one. It is possible to make an artistic judgment that is independent of any question of health or happiness or ordinary morality.

A great artist may paint a picture which shocks all our ordinary ideas of beauty or propriety. He may choose to portray the grotesque, the horrible, the gruesome. He may do this in a way that compels our admiration for his genius. Eliminating, for the time, all other considerations, we may hail it as a masterpiece.

But this does not mean that these other considerations are not to be taken up later on. We might rightfully object to having the picture upon the wall of our living-room, where we should have to look upon the fearful features every day. Because the artist is a genius, shall he be allowed to torture the nerves of an innocent family? That would be to make Art a Moloch demanding human sacrifices.

We admire the skill of a great chemist, but we

do not offer ourselves as his victims. There are
many things in his test tubes which we do not intend to put into our mouths.

From all I have read about them, I have come
to think of the Borgias as a very talented family.
I would give them credit for political ability and
artistic sensibility. They knew a good thing
when they saw it. Yet I should not enjoy taking
a meal with them. I should feel safer to have
honest Bridget prepare my morning coffee.

When we subject ourselves to the influence of
various arts, we have a right to consider their effect upon us. Especially is this true of literature.
We have a right to consider whether what we are
taking into our minds is good for us. A person
may be fortunate enough to have a mind that
is highly resistant to literary suggestion. With
such immunity he is not likely to catch harm
from the most insinuating book. He is like Mith-
ridates who thrived on poison. But one who is
not sure that he possesses a Mithridatic stomach
should exercise a bit of caution.

There was a time when the easiest way to get
rid of high ecclesiastics was by dropping a poison
in consecrated wine. When it was learned by
experience that death might lurk in the sacred

chalice, precautions were taken even by the most pious. And there is no more power in art than in religion to change the nature of things.

But why should one go to works of imagination for a knowledge of facts? If we are interested in engineering, we do not consult a highly colored romance. We prefer a dry textbook by a competent engineer. The sober scientific method does not stimulate the imagination; it curbs it. There are sciences dealing directly with the origin, transmission, and development of life. The facts presented have been tested. There is a technique developed in each science which makes the path of the investigator easy; nothing is conveyed by innuendo. There are specific answers for carefully considered questions.

There is no conspiracy of silence on the part of anthropologists as to primitive customs, and the slow processes by which they have been outgrown. They do not conceal the fact that monogamy has not been the only form of marriage. There is no fear of Mrs. Grundy before their eyes when they trace the steps by which the ethical ideas of civilized man have emerged. Nor is there any conspiracy of silence on the part of physiologists and psychologists. In charting the sea of life they do not conceal the existence of dangerous shoals and treacherous currents. That man has always struggled with an animal inheritance and that his hold on spiritual realities has always been precarious is made evident. Or, if one is seriously interested in morbid states of mind, there is no reason why he should trust to gifted amateurs. There is a well-established science of psychiatry. The scientific treatise has the great advantage that it is written from the standpoint of sanity.

The application of strict laboratory methods to all ethical and social questions would do away, once and for all, with that troublesome question, How far is it safe to go? The answer to that is, Go as far as you can go safely. It is not a question as to the length to which you carry your researches. It is a question as to whether you have adopted the right method of research. You must learn to go step by step, and you must at every step have your feet on firm ground. Then go on as far and as fast as you can.

It is never safe to jump at conclusions. Even a very short jump may lead to intellectual disaster. On the other hand, it is possible for active minds to go far in advance of the multitude, and to come to conclusions that seem strange, and yet never to have deviated from the line of prudence. They have at every moment a perfect awareness of what they are doing. They test everything as they go along. They have the caution which belongs to the man who knows how to experiment. Such minds go far, but as they go they make a safe and broad highway along which the rest of us may travel.

THE END OF THE DELUGE

FIVE years have passed since the end of the World War. Already that war is beginning to take its place as a terrible episode in the history of humanity. What future generations will not realize is the feeling of those who lived through it. Long as the war was, people were unprepared for the end. It caught them unprepared. There was a strange incredulity in the public mind. Peace was like Utopia. Hard-headed people found it difficult to believe that it had actually come. Here in America all our thoughts were on the vast preparations for the coming year. Was it possible that they were no longer needed?

I venture to include in this volume a "parable for the time" written about a fortnight before the Armistice and published in the "Christian Register" November 17, 1918.

SCENE — The Ark. Noah looking out of the window. SHEM, HAM, and JAPHET seated with their backs to the window.

NOAH — I can't see the dove anywhere.

SHEM (*peevishly*) — I said you'd never see that

dove again. And we've lost a perfectly good raven. It's foolish to leave the window open in a time like this.

NOAH — Rejoice, my son, that the dove does not return. It is a sign that the waters of the flood are abating.

SHEM — Last week when the dove came back you said *that* was a good sign.

NOAH (*gently*) — But, my son, you remember it brought us an olive leaf.

SHEM — It was water-soaked. What's an olive leaf in a great flood like this?

NOAH — Cheer up, my son. For forty days and forty nights the windows of heaven were opened, but after that when I looked out I saw signs that made me sure that the waters were abating. Let us accept the good omens. Soon we shall go out again into the pleasant fields.

HAM — That's the trouble with you, father. You are always seeing things. I remember hearing people call you visionary. I didn't know what they meant then, but I know now. You see things before they happen.

NOAH — That's a good way to see them, my son. It gives one time to prepare for them. When I saw that there was going to be a flood I got ready for it. And now that the flood is coming to an end I'm getting ready for that. Come to the window and I'll show you something that will gladden your eyes.

JAPHET — I suppose, father, you expect us to see dry land.

NOAH — I think it is time for you to look for it.

JAPHET — But it would interfere with our work of carrying on the Ark. After we've built an ark like this and filled it with animals you don't think that we're going to give it up just because it has stopped raining. We're going to see this thing through.

HAM — Yes, and we have just been talking of having our children taught so that they can build a bigger and better ark. And if they are to build a bigger ark they must have faith to believe that there will be a bigger flood to float it. You can't neglect the spiritual.

NOAH — But, my son, you must not think that floods go on forever. I lived six hundred years before anything like this happened.

JAPHET — How monotonous the old times were! But let's not talk about the past or the future, but about the present. We are not ante-diluvians or post-diluvians but diluvians. It's a waste of time to talk about anything but the flood. Let us treat it as something permanent.

SHEM — Yes, we must be practical and not delude ourselves with doves and ravens and olive leaves and rainbows. We have been shut up in this ark a long time, and it will be a longer time before we are out of it. We must prepare our minds for that.

> *The Ark gives a sudden lurch, there is a grinding sound, and then all is quiet.*
> SHEM, HAM, *and* JAPHET *are rolled about and then recover themselves.*

SHEM — That was the biggest wave yet! I believe the flood is just beginning. This seems to me like the real thing. As I was saying, father, we must not let hopefulness deceive us. We must all of us face the hard facts.

NOAH (*looking out of the window*) — That's what I am doing. The hard fact is Mount Ararat — and we're on it.

THE END